PSALMS WISDOM

Navigate life wisely with 100+ quotes & proverbs of wisdom, prayer, thanksgiving, trust, praise & worship hymns from the Biblical book of Psalms

By ML James

© 2019 ML James. All rights reserved.

The scripture quotation used in "Introduction" is from the Good News Translation in Today's English Version- Second Edition Copyright © 1992 by American Bible Society. Used by permission.

All other scripture quotations is from New Heart English Bible.

Although every precaution has been taken to verify the accuracy of the information contained herein, the author and publisher assume no responsibility for any errors or omissions. No liability is assumed for damages that may result from the use of information contained within.

AUDIOBOOK OFFER

If you are new to Audible you can get the audiobook version free with a free 30 days Audible trial.

Please follow the below *bit.ly* links based on where you reside.

US: *bit.ly/MLJ_Psalms_US*
UK: *bit.ly/MLJ_Psalms_UK*
France: *bit.ly/MLJ_Psalms_FR*
Germany: *bit.ly/MLJ_Psalms_DE*
All other countries: *bit.ly/MLJ_Psalms_Others*

TABLE OF CONTENTS

INTRODUCTION 9

DEDICATION 10

WISDOM 12

    CHAPTER 1 13
    CHAPTER 2 14
    CHAPTER 3 15
    CHAPTER 4 17
    CHAPTER 5 18
    CHAPTER 6 22
    CHAPTER 7 24
    CHAPTER 8 26
    CHAPTER 9 32
    CHAPTER 10 33
    CHAPTER 11 44
    CHAPTER 12 45
    CHAPTER 13 46
    CHAPTER 14 47

THANKSGIVING 50

    CHAPTER 15 51
    CHAPTER 16 52
    CHAPTER 17 56
    CHAPTER 18 57
    CHAPTER 19 58

CHAPTER 20 59
CHAPTER 21 60
CHAPTER 22 62
CHAPTER 23 64
CHAPTER 24 66
CHAPTER 25 67
CHAPTER 26 69
CHAPTER 27 70
CHAPTER 28 72
CHAPTER 29 73
CHAPTER 30 77
CHAPTER 31 78
CHAPTER 32 79
CHAPTER 33 82
CHAPTER 34 86
CHAPTER 35 89
CHAPTER 36 90
CHAPTER 37 92
CHAPTER 38 94
CHAPTER 39 95
CHAPTER 40 96
CHAPTER 41 97
CHAPTER 42 99
CHAPTER 43 101
CHAPTER 44 102

SONGS & PRAYERS OF TRUST **106**

CHAPTER 45 107
CHAPTER 46 108
CHAPTER 47 109

- CHAPTER 48 110
- CHAPTER 49 112
- CHAPTER 50 114
- CHAPTER 51 115
- CHAPTER 52 116
- CHAPTER 53 117
- CHAPTER 54 118
- CHAPTER 55 120
- CHAPTER 56 121
- CHAPTER 57 122

PRAISE & WORSHIP HYMNS 124

- CHAPTER 58 125
- CHAPTER 59 126
- CHAPTER 60 127
- CHAPTER 61 129
- CHAPTER 62 131
- CHAPTER 63 132
- CHAPTER 64 133
- CHAPTER 65 134
- CHAPTER 66 136
- CHAPTER 67 137
- CHAPTER 68 138
- CHAPTER 69 141
- CHAPTER 70 142
- CHAPTER 71 144
- CHAPTER 72 146
- CHAPTER 73 147
- CHAPTER 74 148
- CHAPTER 75 149

- CHAPTER 76 150
- CHAPTER 77 152
- CHAPTER 78 154
- CHAPTER 79 155
- CHAPTER 80 156
- CHAPTER 81 157
- CHAPTER 82 159
- CHAPTER 83 161
- CHAPTER 84 164
- CHAPTER 85 165
- CHAPTER 86 166
- CHAPTER 87 167
- CHAPTER 88 168
- CHAPTER 89 170
- CHAPTER 90 171
- CHAPTER 91 172
- CHAPTER 92 173
- CHAPTER 93 174
- CHAPTER 94 175
- CHAPTER 95 177
- CHAPTER 96 178
- CHAPTER 97 180
- CHAPTER 98 181
- CHAPTER 99 183
- CHAPTER 100 184
- CHAPTER 101 185

WHAT DID YOU THINK ABOUT PSALMS WITH GOD'S WISDOM 187

OTHER BOOKS TO CONSIDER 188

INTRODUCTION

"Get good advice and you will succeed. Don't go charging into battle without a plan." Proverbs 20:18

- Seeking insights for living life wisely?
- Interested in learning & applying ancient time-tested wisdom?
- Know someone who might benefit from this?

This Christian devotional book contains 100+ thoughtful quotes of wisdom, prayer, thanksgiving, trust, praise & worship hymns from the Biblical book of Psalms that can be great for anyone interested in living wisely.

It can empower, inspire & steer you to do so through:

- Ancient wisdom & instructions in wise dealing.
- Comfort, strength, hope, direction & purpose.
- Discerning the words of understanding.
- Giving shrewdness to the inexperienced.
- Knowledge and discretion to the young.
- Attaining sound counsel.

Get ready to see your life transform over time as you learn, meditate upon & apply the divine wisdom!

DEDICATION

This book is dedicated to my dad.

Dad's been my rock, speaking words of love & wisdom into my life. His words & life inspires, guides and directs my path.

Dad's encouragement to study the Biblical book of Psalms has lead me to write this book.

I love you dad.

WISDOM

CHAPTER 1

Blessed is the one who doesn't follow the advice of the wicked, or take the path of sinners, or join in with scoffers. But his delight is in the law of the LORD, and on his law he meditates day and night.

He will be like a tree planted by the streams of water, that brings forth its fruit in its season, whose leaf also does not wither, and whatever he does shall prosper.

Not so with the wicked; instead, they are like the chaff which the wind drives away from the surface of the ground.

Therefore the wicked shall not stand in the judgment, nor sinners in the congregation of the righteous.

For the LORD knows the way of the righteous, but the way of the wicked shall perish.

PSALM 1

CHAPTER 2

LORD, who shall dwell in your sanctuary? Who shall live on your holy hill? He who walks blamelessly and does what is right, and speaks truth in his heart.

He doesn't slander with his tongue, nor does evil to his friend, nor lifts up an insult against his neighbor. In his eyes a vile man is despised, but he honors those who fear the LORD.

He keeps an oath even when it hurts, and doesn't change it. He doesn't lend out his money for interest, nor takes bribe against the innocent. He who does these things shall never be shaken.

PSALM 15

CHAPTER 3

The heavens declare the glory of God. The expanse shows his handiwork. Day after day they pour forth speech, and night after night they display knowledge.

There is no speech nor language, where their voice is not heard. Their voice has gone out to all the earth, their words to the farthest part of the world.

In them he has set a tent for the sun, which is as a bridegroom coming out of his chamber, like a strong man rejoicing to run his course.

His going forth is from the end of the heavens, his circuit to its ends; There is nothing hidden from its heat.

The LORD's Law is perfect, restoring the soul. The LORD's testimony is sure, making wise the simple. The LORD's precepts are right, rejoicing the heart.

The LORD's commandment is pure, enlightening the eyes. The fear of the LORD is clean, enduring forever. The LORD's ordinances are true, and righteous altogether.

More to be desired are they than gold, yes, than much fine gold; sweeter also than honey and the extract of the honeycomb. Moreover by them is your servant warned.

In keeping them there is great reward. Who can discern his errors?

Forgive me from hidden errors. Keep back your servant also from presumptuous sins. Let them not have dominion over me. Then I will be upright. I will be blameless and innocent of great transgression.

Let the words of my mouth and the meditation of my heart be acceptable in your sight always, LORD, my rock and my redeemer.

PSALM 19

CHAPTER 4

Transgression speaks to the wicked within his heart. There is no fear of God before his eyes. For he flatters himself in his own eyes, too much to detect and hate his sin.

The words of his mouth are iniquity and deceit. He has ceased to be wise and to do good. He plots iniquity on his bed. He sets himself in a way that is not good. He doesn't abhor evil.

Your loving kindness, LORD, is in the heavens. Your faithfulness reaches to the skies. Your righteousness is like the mountains of God. Your judgments are like a great deep. LORD, you preserve man and animal. How precious is your loving kindness, God.

The children of men take refuge under the shadow of your wings. They shall be abundantly satisfied with the abundance of your house. You will make them drink of the river of your pleasures.

For with you is the spring of life. In your light shall we see light. Oh continue your loving kindness to those who know you, your righteousness to the upright in heart.
Do not let the foot of pride come against me. Do not let the hand of the wicked drive me away. There evildoers are fallen. They are thrust down, and shall not be able to rise.

PSALM 36

CHAPTER 5

Do not fret because of evildoers, neither be envious against those who work unrighteousness. For they shall soon be cut down like the grass, and wither like the green herb.

Trust in the LORD, and do good. Dwell in the land, and enjoy safe pasture. Also delight yourself in the LORD, and he will give you the desires of your heart.

Commit your way to the LORD. Trust also in him, and he will act. And he will make your righteousness go forth as the light, and your justice as the noonday.

Rest in the LORD, and wait patiently for him. Do not fret because of him who prospers in his way, because of the man who makes wicked plots happen. Cease from anger, and forsake wrath.

Do not fret, it leads only to evildoing.
For evildoers shall be cut off, but those who wait for the LORD shall inherit the land.

For yet a little while, and the wicked will be no more. Yes, though you look for his place, he isn't there. But the humble shall inherit the land, and shall delight themselves in the abundance of peace.

The wicked plots against the just, and gnashes at him with his teeth. The Lord will laugh at him, for he sees that his day is coming.

The wicked have drawn out the sword, and have bent their bow, to cast down the poor and needy, to kill those who are upright in the way. Their sword shall enter into their own heart. Their bows shall be broken.

Better is a little that the righteous has, than the abundance of many wicked. For the arms of the wicked shall be broken, but the LORD upholds the righteous.

The LORD knows the days of the perfect. Their inheritance shall be forever. They shall not be disappointed in the time of evil. In the days of famine they shall be satisfied. But the wicked shall perish.

The enemies of the LORD shall be like the beauty of the fields. They will vanish – vanish like smoke. The wicked borrow, and do not pay back, but the righteous give generously.

For such as are blessed by him shall inherit the land. Those who are cursed by him shall be cut off. The steps of a man are established by the LORD, and he delights in his way. Though he stumble, he shall not fall, for the LORD holds him up with his hand.

I have been young, and now am old, yet I have not seen the righteous forsaken, nor his children begging for bread. All day long he deals graciously and lends, and his offspring are a blessing.

Turn away from evil, and do good. Live securely forever. For the LORD loves justice, and doesn't forsake his faithful ones. They are preserved forever, but the children of the wicked shall be cut off.

The righteous shall inherit the land, and live in it forever. The mouth of the righteous talks of wisdom. His tongue speaks justice.

The law of his God is in his heart. None of his steps shall slide. The wicked watches the righteous, and seeks to kill him. The LORD will not leave him in his hand, nor condemn him when he is judged.

Wait for the LORD, and keep his way, and he will exalt you to inherit the land. When the wicked are cut off, you shall see it. I have seen the wicked in great power, spreading himself like a green tree in its native soil.

But he passed away, and look, he was not. Yes, I sought him, but he could not be found.

Observe the blameless, and see the upright, for there is a future for the man of peace. As for transgressors, they shall be destroyed together. The future of the wicked shall be cut off.

The salvation of the righteous is from the LORD. He is their stronghold in the time of trouble. And the LORD helps them, and rescues them.

He rescues them from the wicked, and saves them, because they have taken refuge in him.

PSALM 37

CHAPTER 6

Hear this, all you peoples. Listen, all you inhabitants of the world, both low and high, rich and poor together. My mouth will speak words of wisdom.

My heart shall utter understanding. I will incline my ear to a proverb. I will open my riddle on the harp.

Why should I fear in the days of evil, when iniquity at my heels surrounds me? Those who trust in their wealth, and boast in the multitude of their riches — none of them can by any means redeem his brother, nor give God a ransom for him.

For the redemption of their life is costly, no payment is ever enough, that he should live on forever, that he should not see corruption.

For he sees that wise men die; likewise the fool and the senseless perish, and leave their wealth to others. Their tombs are their homes forever, and their dwelling places to all generations. They name their lands after themselves.

But man, despite his riches, doesn't endure. He is like the animals that perish. This is the destiny of those who are foolish, and of those who approve their sayings. Selah.

They are appointed as a flock for Sheol. Death shall be their shepherd. The upright shall have dominion over them in the morning.

Their beauty shall decay in Sheol, far from their mansion. But God will redeem my soul from the power of Sheol, for he will receive me. Selah.

Do not be afraid when a man is made rich, when the glory of his house is increased. For when he dies he shall carry nothing away.

His glory shall not descend after him. Though while he lived he blessed his soul – and men praise you when you do well for yourself – he shall go to the generation of his fathers. They shall never see the light.

A man who has riches without understanding, is like the animals that perish.

PSALM 49

CHAPTER 7

Surely God is good to Israel, to those who are pure in heart. But as for me, my feet were almost gone. My steps had nearly slipped. For I was envious of the arrogant, when I saw the prosperity of the wicked.

For there are no struggles in their death, but their strength is firm. They are free from burdens of men, neither are they plagued like other men. Therefore pride is like a chain around their neck.

Violence covers them like a garment. Their sin proceeds forth from fatness. Their hearts overflow with imaginations. They scoff and speak with malice. In arrogance, they threaten oppression.

They have set their mouth in the heavens. Their tongue walks through the earth. Therefore my people turn to them, and they drink up waters of abundance.

They say, "How does God know? Is there knowledge in the Most High?" Look, these are the wicked. Being always at ease, they increase in riches.

Surely in vain I have cleansed my heart, and washed my hands in innocence, for all day long have I been plagued, and punished every morning.

If I had said, "I will speak thus;" look, I would have betrayed the generation of your children. When I tried to understand this, it was too painful for me; until I entered God's sanctuary, and considered their latter end.

Surely you set them in slippery places. You throw them down to destruction. How they are suddenly destroyed. They are completely swept away with terrors.

As a dream when one wakes up, so, Lord, when you awake, you will despise their fantasies. For my soul was grieved. I was embittered in my heart.

I was so senseless and ignorant. I was a brute beast before you. Nevertheless, I am continually with you. You have held my right hand. You will guide me with your counsel, and afterward receive me to glory.

Who do I have in heaven? There is no one on earth who I desire besides you. My flesh and my heart fails, but God is the strength of my heart and my portion forever. For, look, those who are far from you shall perish. You have destroyed all those who are unfaithful to you.

But it is good for me to come close to God. I have made the LORD my refuge, that I may tell of all your works in the gates of the daughter of Zion.

PSALM 73

CHAPTER 8

Hear my teaching, my people. Turn your ears to the words of my mouth. I will open my mouth in parables. I will utter dark sayings of old, which we have heard and known, and our fathers have told us.

We will not hide them from their children, telling to the generation to come the praises of the LORD, his strength, and his wondrous works that he has done.

For he established a testimony in Jacob, and appointed a teaching in Israel, which he commanded our fathers, that they should make them known to their children; that the generation to come might know it, the children yet unborn, and arise and tell their children, that they might set their hope in God, and not forget the works of God, but keep his commandments, and might not be as their fathers, a stubborn and rebellious generation, a generation that did not make their hearts loyal, whose spirit was not steadfast with God.

The children of Ephraim, being armed and carrying bows, turned back in the day of battle. They did not keep God's covenant, and refused to walk by his Law. They forgot his doings, his wondrous works that he had shown them.

He did marvelous things in the sight of their fathers, in the land of Egypt, in the field of Zoan. He split the sea, and caused them to pass through. He made the waters stand as a heap. In the daytime he also led them with a cloud, and all night with a light of fire.

He split rocks in the wilderness, and gave them drink abundantly as out of the depths. He brought streams also out of the rock, and caused waters to run down like rivers. Yet they still went on to sin against him, to rebel against the Most High in the desert.

They tempted God in their heart by asking food according to their desire. Yes, they spoke against God. They said, "Can God prepare a table in the wilderness?

Look, he struck the rock, so that waters gushed out, and streams overflowed. Can he give bread also? Will he provide flesh for his people?"

Therefore the LORD heard, and was angry. A fire was kindled against Jacob, anger also went up against Israel, because they did not believe in God, and did not trust in his salvation.

Yet he commanded the clouds above, and opened the doors of heaven. He rained down manna on them to eat, and gave them bread from heaven. Man ate the bread of angels. He sent them food to the full.

He caused the east wind to blow in the sky. By his power he guided the south wind. He rained also flesh on them as the dust; winged birds as the sand of the seas.

He let them fall in the midst of their camp, around their habitations. So they ate, and were well filled. He gave them their own desire. They did not turn from their cravings.

Their food was yet in their mouths, when the anger of God went up against them, killed some of the fattest of them, and struck down the young men of Israel.

For all this they still sinned, and did not believe in his wondrous works. Therefore he consumed their days in vanity, and their years in terror.

When he killed them, then they inquired after him. They returned and sought God earnestly. They remembered that God was their rock, the Most High God, their redeemer. But they flattered him with their mouth, and lied to him with their tongue.

For their heart was not right with him, neither were they faithful in his covenant. But he, being merciful, forgave iniquity, and did not destroy them.

Yes, many times he turned his anger away, and did not stir up all his wrath. He remembered that they were but flesh, a wind that passes away, and doesn't come again.

How often they rebelled against him in the wilderness, and grieved him in the desert. They turned again and tempted God, and gave pain to the Holy One of Israel.

They did not remember his hand, nor the day when he redeemed them from the adversary; how he set his signs in Egypt, his wonders in the field of Zoan, he turned their rivers into blood, and their streams, so that they could not drink.

He sent among them swarms of flies, which devoured them; and frogs, which destroyed them. He gave also their increase to the caterpillar, and their labor to the locust.

He destroyed their vines with hail, their sycamore fig trees with frost. He gave over their livestock also to the hail, and their flocks to hot thunderbolts.

He threw on them the fierceness of his anger, wrath, indignation, and trouble, and a band of destroying angels. He made a path for his anger.

He did not spare their soul from death, but gave their life over to the pestilence, and struck all the firstborn in Egypt, the chief of their strength in the tents of Ham.

But he led forth his own people like sheep, and guided them in the wilderness like a flock. He led them safely, so that they weren't afraid, but the sea overwhelmed their enemies.

He brought them to the border of his sanctuary, to this mountain, which his right hand had taken.

He also drove out the nations before them, allotted them for an inheritance by line, and made the tribes of Israel to dwell in their tents.

Yet they tempted and rebelled against the Most High God, and did not keep his testimonies; but turned back, and dealt treacherously like their fathers. They were turned aside like a deceitful bow.

For they provoked him to anger with their high places, and moved him to jealousy with their engraved images. When God heard this, he was angry, and greatly abhorred Israel;

So that he forsook the tabernacle at Shiloh, the tent where he dwelt among men; and delivered his strength into captivity, his glory into the adversary's hand.

He also gave his people over to the sword, and was angry with his inheritance. Fire devoured their young men. Their virgins had no wedding song. Their priests fell by the sword, and their widows couldn't weep.

Then the Lord awakened as one out of sleep, like a mighty man who shouts by reason of wine. He struck his adversaries backward. He put them to a perpetual reproach.

Moreover he rejected the tent of Joseph, and did not choose the tribe of Ephraim, but chose the tribe of Judah, Mount Zion which he loved. He built his sanctuary like the heights, like the earth which he has established forever.

He also chose David his servant, and took him from the sheepfolds; from following the ewes that have their young, he brought him to be the shepherd of Jacob his servant, and Israel his inheritance.

So he was their shepherd according to the integrity of his heart, and guided them by the skillfulness of his hands.

PSALM 78

CHAPTER 9

Praise the LORD. Blessed is the man who fears the LORD, who delights greatly in his commandments. His descendants will be mighty in the land.

The generation of the upright will be blessed. Wealth and riches are in his house. His righteousness endures forever. Light dawns in the darkness for the upright, gracious, merciful, and righteous.

It is well with the man who deals graciously and lends. He will maintain his cause in judgment. For he will never be shaken. The righteous will be remembered forever.

He will not be afraid of evil news. His heart is steadfast, trusting in the LORD.

His heart is secure, he has no fears; in the end he will look in triumph on his adversaries. He has scattered, he has given to the poor; his righteousness endures forever. His horn will be exalted with honor.

The wicked will see it, and be grieved. He shall gnash with his teeth, and melt away. The desire of the wicked will perish.

PSALM 112

CHAPTER 10

Blessed are those whose ways are blameless, who walk according to the law of the LORD. Blessed are those who keep his decrees, who seek him with their whole heart.

Yes, they do nothing wrong. They walk in his ways. You have commanded your precepts, that we should fully obey them. Oh that my ways were steadfast to obey your statutes.

Then I wouldn't be disappointed, when I consider all of your commandments. I will give thanks to you with uprightness of heart, when I learn your righteous judgments. I will observe your statutes.

Do not utterly forsake me. How can a young man keep his way pure? By living according to your word. With my whole heart, I have sought you.

Do not let me wander from your commandments. In my heart I have hidden your word, that I might not sin against you.

Blessed are you, LORD. Teach me your statutes. With my lips, I have declared all the ordinances of your mouth. I have rejoiced in the way of your testimonies, as much as in all riches.

I will meditate on your precepts, and consider your ways. I will delight myself in your statutes. I will not forget your words.

Deal bountifully with your servant, that I may live and keep your words. Open my eyes, that I may see wondrous things out of your Law. I am a stranger on the earth. Do not hide your commandments from me.

My soul is consumed with longing for your ordinances at all times. You have rebuked the proud who are cursed, who wander from your commandments.

Take reproach and contempt away from me, for I have kept your statutes. Though princes sit and slander me, your servant will meditate on your statutes. Indeed your statutes are my delight, and my counselors.

My soul is laid low in the dust. Revive me according to your word. I declared my ways, and you answered me. Teach me your statutes. Let me understand the teaching of your precepts. Then I will meditate on your wondrous works.

My soul is weary with sorrow: strengthen me according to your word. Keep me from the way of deceit. Grant me your Law graciously. I have chosen the way of truth. I have set your ordinances before me.

I cling to your statutes, LORD. Do not let me be disappointed. I run in the path of your commandments, for you have set my heart free. HEY Teach me, LORD, the way of your statutes. I will keep them to the end.

Give me understanding, and I will keep your Law. Yes, I will obey it with my whole heart. Direct me in the path of your commandments, for I delight in them.

Turn my heart toward your statutes, not toward selfish gain. Turn my eyes away from looking at worthless things. Revive me in your ways. Fulfill your promise to your servant, that you may be feared.

Take away my disgrace that I dread, for your ordinances are good. Look, I long for your precepts. Revive me in your righteousness.

Let your loving kindness also come to me, LORD, your salvation, according to your word. So I will have an answer for him who reproaches me, for I trust in your word.

Do not snatch the word of truth out of my mouth, for I put my hope in your ordinances.

So I will obey your Law continually, forever and ever. I will walk in liberty, for I have sought your precepts. I will also speak of your statutes before kings, and will not be disappointed.

I will delight myself in your commandments, because I love them. I reach out my hands for your commandments, which I love.

I will meditate on your statutes. Remember your word to your servant, because you gave me hope. This is my comfort in my affliction, for your word has revived me. The arrogant mock me excessively, but I do not swerve from your Law.

I remember your ordinances of old, LORD, and have comforted myself. Indignation has taken hold on me, because of the wicked who forsake your Law. Your statutes have been my songs, in the house where I live.

I have remembered your name, LORD, in the night, and I obey your Law. This is my way, that I keep your precepts. The LORD is my portion. I promised to obey your words.

I sought your favor with my whole heart. Be merciful to me according to your word. I considered my ways, and turned my steps to your statutes.

I will hurry, and not delay, to obey your commandments. The ropes of the wicked bind me, but I won't forget your Law.

At midnight I will rise to give thanks to you, because of your righteous ordinances. I am a friend of all those who fear you, of those who observe your precepts. The earth is full of your loving kindness, LORD. Teach me your statutes.

Do good to your servant, according to your word, LORD. Teach me good judgment and knowledge, for I believe in your commandments.

Before I was afflicted, I went astray; but now I observe your word. You are good, and do good. Teach me your statutes.

The proud have smeared a lie upon me. With my whole heart, I will keep your precepts. Their heart is as callous as the fat, but I delight in your Law. It is good for me that I have been afflicted, that I may learn your statutes.

The Law you have spoken is better to me than thousands of pieces of gold and silver. YOD Your hands have made me and formed me. Give me understanding, that I may learn your commandments.

Those who fear you will see me and be glad, because I have put my hope in your word. LORD, I know that your judgments are righteous, that in faithfulness you have humbled me.

Please let your loving kindness be for my comfort, according to your word to your servant. Let your tender mercies come to me, that I may live; for your Law is my delight.

Let the proud be disappointed, for they have overthrown me wrongfully.

I will meditate on your precepts. Let those who fear you turn to me. They will know your statutes. Let my heart be blameless toward your decrees, that I may not be disappointed.

My soul faints for your salvation. I hope in your word. My eyes fail for your word. I say, "When will you comfort me?" For I have become like a wineskin in the smoke.

I do not forget your statutes. How many are the days of your servant? When will you execute judgment on those who persecute me?

The proud have dug pits for me, contrary to your Law. All of your commandments are faithful.

They persecute me wrongfully. Help me. They had almost wiped me from the earth, but I did not forsake your precepts. Preserve my life according to your loving kindness, so I will obey the statutes of your mouth.

LORD, your word is settled in heaven forever. Your faithfulness is to all generations. You have established the earth, and it remains. Your laws remain to this day, for all things serve you.

Unless your Law had been my delight, I would have perished in my affliction. I will never forget your precepts, for with them, you have revived me. I am yours. Save me, for I have sought your precepts.

The wicked have waited for me, to destroy me. I will consider your statutes. I have seen a limit to all perfection, but your commands are boundless.

How I love your Law. It is my meditation all day. Your commandments make me wiser than my enemies, for your commandments are always with me.

I have more understanding than all my teachers, for your testimonies are my meditation. I understand more than the aged, because I have kept your precepts.

I have kept my feet from every evil way, that I might observe your word. I have not turned aside from your ordinances, for you have taught me. How sweet are your promises to my taste, more than honey to my mouth.

Through your precepts, I get understanding; therefore I hate every false way. Your word is a lamp to my feet, and a light for my path.

I have sworn, and have confirmed it, that I will obey your righteous ordinances. I am afflicted very much.

Revive me, LORD, according to your word. Please accept the freewill offerings of my mouth, LORD, and teach me your ordinances.

My soul is continually in my hand, yet I won't forget your Law. The wicked have laid a snare for me, yet I haven't gone astray from your precepts.

I have taken your testimonies as a heritage forever, for they are the joy of my heart. I have set my heart to perform your statutes forever, even to the end.

I hate double-minded men, but I love your Law. You are my hiding place and my shield. I hope in your word. Depart from me, you evildoers, that I may keep the commandments of my God.

Uphold me according to your word, that I may live. Let me not be ashamed of my hope. Hold me up, and I will be safe, and will have respect for your statutes continually.

You reject all those who stray from your statutes, for their deceit is in vain.

You put away all the wicked of the earth like dross. Therefore I love your testimonies. My flesh trembles for fear of you. I am afraid of your judgments.

I have done what is just and righteous. Do not leave me to my oppressors. Ensure your servant's well-being. Do not let the proud oppress me.

My eyes fail looking for your salvation, for your righteous word. Deal with your servant according to your loving kindness.

Teach me your statutes. I am your servant. Give me understanding, that I may know your testimonies. It is time to act, LORD, for they break your Law.

Therefore I love your commandments more than gold, yes, more than pure gold. Therefore I consider all of your precepts to be right. I hate every false way.

Your testimonies are wonderful, therefore my soul keeps them. The entrance of your words gives light. It gives understanding to the simple. I opened my mouth wide and panted, for I longed for your commandments.

Turn to me, and have mercy on me, as you always do to those who love your name. Establish my footsteps in your word. Do not let any iniquity have dominion over me. Redeem me from the oppression of man, so I will observe your precepts.

Make your face shine on your servant. Teach me your statutes. Streams of tears run down my eyes, because they do not observe your Law.

You are righteous, LORD. Your judgments are upright. You have commanded your statutes in righteousness. They are fully trustworthy. My zeal wears me out, because my enemies ignore your words.

Your promises have been thoroughly tested, and your servant loves them. I am small and despised. I do not forget your precepts. Your righteousness is an everlasting righteousness.

Your Law is truth. Trouble and anguish have taken hold of me. Your commandments are my delight. Your testimonies are righteous forever. Give me understanding, that I may live.

I have called with my whole heart. Answer me, LORD. I will keep your statutes. I have called to you. Save me. I will obey your statutes.

I rise before dawn and cry for help. I put my hope in your words. My eyes stay open through the night watches, that I might meditate on your word.

Hear my voice according to your loving kindness. Revive me, LORD, according to your ordinances. They draw near who follow after wickedness. They are far from your Law.

You are near, LORD. All your commandments are truth. Of old I have known from your testimonies, that you have founded them forever.

Consider my affliction, and deliver me, for I do not forget your Law. Plead my cause, and redeem me. Revive me according to your promise. Salvation is far from the wicked, for they do not seek your statutes.

Great are your tender mercies, LORD. Revive me according to your ordinances. Many are my persecutors and my adversaries.

I haven't swerved from your testimonies. I look at the faithless with loathing, because they do not observe your word. Consider how I love your precepts.

Revive me, LORD, according to your loving kindness. All of your words are truth. Every one of your righteous ordinances endures forever.

Princes have persecuted me without a cause, but my heart stands in awe of your words. I rejoice at your word, as one who finds great spoil. I hate and abhor falsehood. I love your Law.

Seven times a day, I praise you, because of your righteous ordinances. Those who love your Law have great peace. Nothing causes them to stumble. I have hoped for your salvation, LORD. I have done your commandments.

My soul has observed your testimonies. I love them exceedingly. I have obeyed your precepts and your testimonies, for all my ways are before you.

Let my cry come before you, LORD. Give me understanding according to your word.

Let my petition come before you. Deliver me according to your word. Let my lips utter praise, for you teach me your statutes. Let my tongue sing of your word, for all your commandments are righteousness.

Let your hand be ready to help me, for I have chosen your precepts. I have longed for your salvation, LORD. Your Law is my delight.

Let my soul live, that I may praise you. Let your ordinances help me. I have gone astray like a lost sheep. Seek your servant, for I do not forget your commandments.

PSALM 119

CHAPTER 11

Unless the LORD builds the house, they labor in vain who build it. Unless the LORD watches over the city, the watchman guards it in vain.

It is vain for you to rise up early, to stay up late, eating the bread of toil; for he gives sleep to his loved ones. Look, children are a heritage of the LORD. The fruit of the womb is his reward.

As arrows in the hand of a mighty man, so are the children of youth. Blessed is the man who has his quiver full of them.

They won't be disappointed when they speak with their enemies in the gate.

PSALM 127

CHAPTER 12

Blessed is everyone who fears the LORD, who walks in his ways. For you will eat the labor of your hands; you will be blessed, and it will be well with you.

Your wife will be as a fruitful vine, in the innermost parts of your house; your children like olive plants, around your table.

Look, thus is the man blessed who fears the LORD. May the LORD bless you out of Zion, and may you see the good of Jerusalem all the days of your life.

Yes, may you see your children's children. Peace be upon Israel.

PSALM 128

CHAPTER 13

See how good and how pleasant it is for brothers to live together in unity.

It is like the precious oil on the head, that ran down on the beard, even Aaron's beard; that came down on the edge of his robes; like the dew of Hermon, that comes down on the hills of Zion: for there the LORD gives the blessing, even life forevermore.

PSALM 133

CHAPTER 14

LORD, you have searched me, and you know me. You know my sitting down and my rising up. You perceive my thoughts from afar.

You search out my path and my lying down, and are acquainted with all my ways. For there is not a word on my tongue, but, look, LORD, you know it altogether.

You encircle me behind and in front, and you place your hand upon me. This knowledge is beyond me. It's lofty. I can't attain it. Where could I go from your Spirit? Or where could I flee from your presence?

If I ascend up into heaven, you are there. If I make my bed in Sheol, look, you are there. If I take the wings of the dawn, and settle in the uttermost parts of the sea; even there your hand will lead me, and your right hand will hold me.

If I say, "Surely the darkness will overwhelm me; the light around me will be night;" even the darkness doesn't hide from you, but the night shines as the day. The darkness is like light to you.

For you formed my inmost being. You knit me together in my mother's womb. I will give thanks to you, for I am awesomely and wonderfully made. Your works are wonderful. My soul knows that very well.

My frame wasn't hidden from you, when I was made in secret, woven together in the depths of the earth. Your eyes saw my body. In your book they were all written, the days that were ordained for me, when as yet there were none of them.

How precious to me are your thoughts, God. How vast is the sum of them. If I would count them, they are more in number than the sand. When I wake up, I am still with you. If only you, God, would kill the wicked.

Get away from me, you bloodthirsty men. For they speak against you wickedly. Your enemies take your name in vain. LORD, do I not hate those who hate you? Am I not grieved with those who rise up against you?

I hate them with perfect hatred. They have become my enemies. Search me, God, and know my heart. Try me, and know my thoughts. See if there is any wicked way in me, and lead me in the everlasting way.

PSALM 139

THANKSGIVING

CHAPTER 15

Why do the nations rage, and the peoples plot in vain? The kings of the earth take a stand, and the rulers take counsel together, against the LORD, and against his Anointed:

"Let's tear off their shackles, and throw off their ropes from us." The one who sits in the heavens laughs. The LORD scoffs at them. Then he will speak to them in his anger, and terrify them in his wrath: "But I myself have installed my king on Zion, my holy hill."

I will tell of the decree. The LORD said to me, "You are my son. Today I have become your father. Ask of me, and I will give the nations as your inheritance, and the farthest parts of the earth for your possession.

You shall rule them with an iron scepter. You shall dash them in pieces like a potter's vessel." Now therefore, you kings, be wise; receive correction, you judges of the earth. Serve the LORD with fear, and rejoice with trembling.

Do homage in purity, lest he be angry, and you perish in the way, when his anger is suddenly kindled. Blessed are all those who take refuge in him.

PSALM 2

CHAPTER 16

I love you, LORD, my strength. The LORD is my Rock, my fortress, and my deliverer; my God, my Rock, in whom I take refuge; my shield, and the horn of my salvation, my high tower.

I call on the LORD, who is worthy to be praised; and I am saved from my enemies. The cords of death surrounded me. The floods of ungodliness made me afraid. The cords of Sheol were around me. The snares of death came on me.

In my distress I called on the LORD, and cried to my God. He heard my voice out of his temple. My cry before him came into his ears. Then the earth shook and trembled. The foundations also of the mountains quaked and were shaken, because he was angry.

Smoke went out of his nostrils. Consuming fire came out of his mouth. Coals were kindled by it. He bowed the heavens also, and came down.

Thick darkness was under his feet. He rode on a cherub, and flew. Yes, he soared on the wings of the wind. He made darkness his hiding place, his pavilion around him, darkness of waters, thick clouds of the skies. At the brightness before him his thick clouds passed, hailstones and coals of fire. The LORD also thundered in the sky.

The Most High uttered his voice: hailstones and coals of fire. He sent out his arrows, and scattered them; and he multiplied lightnings, and routed them.

And the depths of the sea appeared. The foundations of the world were laid bare at your rebuke, LORD, at the blast of the breath of your nostrils.

He sent from on high. He took me. He drew me out of many waters. He delivered me from my strong enemy, from those who hated me; for they were too mighty for me. They came on me in the day of my calamity, but the LORD was my support.

He brought me forth also into a large place. He delivered me, because he delighted in me. The LORD has rewarded me according to my righteousness. According to the cleanness of my hands has he recompensed me.

For I have kept the ways of the LORD, and have not wickedly departed from my God. For all his ordinances were before me. I did not put away his statutes from me. I was also blameless with him. I kept myself from my iniquity.

Therefore the LORD has rewarded me according to my righteousness, according to the cleanness of my hands in his eyesight. With the faithful you show yourself faithful. With the blameless man you show yourself blameless.

With the pure you show yourself pure. And with the crooked you show yourself tortuous. For you will save the afflicted people, but the haughty eyes you will bring down.

For you will light my lamp, LORD. My God will light up my darkness. For by you, I advance through a troop. By my God, I leap over a wall.

As for God, his way is perfect. The word of the LORD is pure. He is a shield to all those who take refuge in him. For who is God, except the LORD? Who is a rock, besides our God, the God who girds me with strength, and makes my way perfect?

He makes my feet like deer's feet, and sets me on my high places. He teaches my hands to war, so that my arms bend a bow of bronze. You have also given me the shield of your salvation.

Your right hand sustains me. Your gentleness has made me great. You have enlarged my steps under me, my feet have not slipped. I will pursue my enemies, and overtake them. Neither will I turn again until they are consumed.

I will strike them through, so that they will not be able to rise. They shall fall under my feet. For you have girded me with strength to the battle. You have subdued under me those who rose up against me. You have also made my enemies turn their backs to me, that I might cut off those who hate me.

They cried, but there was none to save; even to the LORD, but he did not answer them. Then I beat them small as the dust before the wind. I trample them like the mud of the streets.

You have delivered me from the strivings of the people. You have made me the head of the nations. A people whom I have not known shall serve me. As soon as they hear of me they shall obey me.

The foreigners shall submit themselves to me. The foreigners shall fade away, and shall come trembling out of their close places. The LORD lives; and blessed be my rock. Exalted be the God of my salvation, even the God who executes vengeance for me, and subdues peoples under me.

He rescues me from my enemies. Yes, you lift me up above those who rise up against me. You deliver me from the violent man.

Therefore I will praise you, LORD, among the nations, and will sing praises to your name. He gives great deliverance to his king, and shows loving kindness to his anointed, to David and to his descendants, until forever.

PSALM 18

CHAPTER 17

May the LORD answer you in the day of trouble. May the name of the God of Jacob set you up on high. He will send you help from the sanctuary, and give you support from Zion.

He will remember all your offerings, and accept your burnt sacrifice. Selah. He will grant you your heart's desire, and fulfill all your plans. We will triumph in your salvation. In the name of our God, we will set up our banners. May the LORD grant all your requests.

Now I know that the LORD saves his anointed. He will answer him from his holy heaven, with the saving strength of his right hand. Some [trust] in chariots, and some in horses, but we trust the name of the LORD our God.

They are bowed down and fallen, but we rise up, and stand upright. Save, LORD. Let the King answer us when we call.

PSALM 20

CHAPTER 18

The king rejoices in your strength, LORD. How greatly he rejoices in your salvation. You have given him his heart's desire, and have not withheld the request of his lips. Selah. For you meet him with the blessings of goodness.

You set a crown of fine gold on his head. He asked life of you, you gave it to him, even length of days forever and ever. His glory is great in your salvation. You lay honor and majesty on him.

For you make him most blessed forever. You make him glad with joy in your presence. For the king trusts in the LORD. Through the loving kindness of the Most High, he shall not be moved. Your hand will find out all of your enemies. Your right hand will find all those who hate you.

You will make them as a fiery furnace in the time of your anger. The LORD will swallow them up in his wrath. The fire shall devour them. You will destroy their descendants from the earth, their posterity from among the children of men. For they intended evil against you.

They plotted evil against you which cannot succeed. For you will make them turn their back, when you aim drawn bows at their face. Be exalted, LORD, in your strength, so we will sing and praise your power.

PSALM 21

CHAPTER 19

I will extol you, LORD, for you have raised me up, and have not made my foes to rejoice over me. LORD my God, I cried to you, and you have healed me. LORD, you have brought up my soul from Sheol.

You have kept me alive, that I should not go down to the pit. Sing praise to the LORD, you his faithful ones. Give thanks to his holy name. For his anger is but for a moment. His favor is for a lifetime. Weeping may stay for the night, but joy comes in the morning.

As for me, I said in my prosperity, "I shall never be moved." You, LORD, when you favored me, made my mountain stand strong; but when you hid your face, I was troubled. I cried to you, LORD. To the Lord I made petition:

"What profit is there in my destruction, if I go down to the pit? Shall the dust praise you? Shall it declare your truth? Hear, LORD, and have mercy on me. LORD, be my helper."

You have turned my mourning into dancing for me. You have removed my sackcloth, and clothed me with gladness, to the end that my heart may sing praise to you, and not be silent. LORD my God, I will give thanks to you forever.

PSALM 30

CHAPTER 20

Happy are those whose transgressions are forgiven, and whose sins are covered. Happy is the one to whom the LORD does not charge with sin, in whose spirit there is no deceit.

When I kept silence, my bones wasted away through my groaning all day long. For day and night your hand was heavy on me. My strength was sapped in the heat of summer. Selah. I acknowledged my sin to you.

I did not hide my iniquity. I said, I will confess my transgressions to the LORD, and you forgave the iniquity of my sin. Selah. For this, let everyone who is faithful pray to you in a time when you may be found. Surely when the great waters overflow, they shall not reach to him.

You are my hiding place. You will preserve me from trouble. You will surround me with songs of deliverance. Selah. I will instruct you and teach you in the way which you shall go. I will counsel you with my eye on you.

Do not be like the horse, or like the mule, which have no understanding, who are controlled by bit and bridle, or else they will not come near to you. Many sorrows come to the wicked, but loving kindness shall surround him who trusts in the LORD. Be glad in the LORD, and rejoice, you righteous. Shout for joy, all you who are upright in heart.

PSALM 32

CHAPTER 21

I will bless the LORD at all times. His praise will always be in my mouth. My soul shall boast in the LORD. The humble shall hear of it, and be glad. Oh magnify the LORD with me. Let us exalt his name together.

I sought the LORD, and he answered me, and delivered me from all my fears. They looked to him and were radiant, and their faces are not ashamed. This poor man cried, and the LORD heard him, and saved him out of all his troubles.

The angel of the LORD encamps around those who fear him, and delivers them. Oh taste and see that the LORD is good. Blessed is the man who takes refuge in him. Oh fear the LORD, you his holy ones, for there is no lack with those who fear him.

The young lions do lack, and suffer hunger, but those who seek the LORD shall not lack any good thing. Come, you children, listen to me. I will teach you the fear of the LORD.

Who is someone who desires life, and loves many days, that he may see good? Keep your tongue from evil, and your lips from speaking lies. Turn away from evil, and do good. Seek peace, and pursue it. The eyes of the LORD are toward the righteous.

His ears listen to their cry. The LORD's face is against those who do evil, to cut off the memory of them from the earth. The righteous cry out, and the LORD hears, and delivers them out of all their troubles.

The LORD is near to those who have a broken heart, and saves those who have a crushed spirit. Many are the afflictions of the righteous, but the LORD delivers him out of them all.

He protects all of his bones. Not one of them is broken. Evil shall kill the wicked. Those who hate the righteous shall be condemned. The LORD redeems the soul of his servants. None of those who take refuge in him shall be condemned.

PSALM 34

CHAPTER 22

I waited patiently for the LORD, and he turned to me, and heard my cry. He also brought me up out of a pit of tumult, out of the miry clay; and he set my feet on a rock, making my steps secure.

And he has put a new song in my mouth, even praise to our God. Many shall see it, and fear, and shall trust in the LORD. Blessed is the man who makes the LORD his trust, and doesn't respect the proud, nor such as turn aside to lies.

Many, LORD, my God, are the wonderful works which you have done, and your thoughts which are toward us. They can't be declared back to you.

If I would declare and speak of them, they are more than can be numbered. Sacrifice and offering you did not desire, but a body you prepared for me. Whole burnt offering and sin offering you did not require.

Then I said, "Look, I have come. It is written about me in the scroll of a book; to do your will, my God, I desired. And your Law is within my heart." I have proclaimed glad news of righteousness in the great assembly. Look, I will not seal my lips, LORD, you know.

I have not hidden your righteousness within my heart. I have declared your faithfulness and your salvation. I have not concealed your loving kindness and your truth from the great assembly. Do not withhold your tender mercies from me, LORD.

Let your loving kindness and your truth continually preserve me. For innumerable evils have surrounded me. My iniquities have overtaken me, so that I am not able to look up. They are more than the hairs of my head. My heart has failed me. Be pleased, LORD, to deliver me.

Hurry to help me, LORD. Let them be disappointed and confounded together who seek after my soul to destroy it. Let them be turned backward and brought to dishonor who delight in my hurt.

Let them be desolate by reason of their shame that tell me, "Aha. Aha." Let all those who seek you rejoice and be glad in you. Let such as love your salvation say continually, "Let the LORD be exalted."

But I am poor and needy. May the Lord think about me. You are my help and my deliverer. Do not delay, my God.

PSALM 40

CHAPTER 23

My heart overflows with a noble theme. I recite my verses for the king. My tongue is like the pen of a skillful writer. You are the most excellent of the sons of men. Grace has anointed your lips, therefore God has blessed you forever. Gird your sword on your thigh, mighty one: your splendor and your majesty.

In your majesty ride on victoriously on behalf of truth, humility, and righteousness. Let your right hand display awesome deeds. Your arrows are sharp. The nations fall under you, with arrows in the heart of the king's enemies. Your throne, God, is forever and ever. A scepter of equity is the scepter of your kingdom.

You have loved righteousness, and hated wickedness. Therefore God, your God, has anointed you with the oil of gladness above your companions. All your garments smell like myrrh and aloes and cassia. Out of ivory palaces stringed instruments have made you glad. Kings' daughters are among your honorable women.

At your right hand the queen stands in gold of Ophir. Listen, daughter, consider, and turn your ear. Forget your own people, and also your father's house. So the king will desire your beauty, honor him, for he is your lord.

The daughter of Tyre comes with a gift. The rich among the people will seek your favor. The princess inside is all glorious. Her clothing is interwoven with gold. She shall be led to the king in embroidered work. The virgins, her companions who follow her, shall be brought to you.

With gladness and rejoicing they shall be led. They shall enter into the king's palace. Your sons will take the place of your fathers. You shall make them princes in all the earth.

I will make your name to be remembered in all generations. Therefore the peoples shall give you thanks forever and ever.

PSALM 45

CHAPTER 24

Praise awaits you, God, in Zion. And to you shall vows be performed. You who hear prayer, to you all men will come. Sins overwhelmed me, but you atoned for our transgressions. Blessed is the one you choose and bring near, that he may dwell in your courts. We will be filled with the goodness of your house, your holy temple. By awesome deeds of righteousness, you answer us, God of our salvation. You who are the hope of every part of the earth, of those who are far away on the sea;

Who by his power forms the mountains, having armed yourself with strength; who stills the roaring of the seas, the roaring of their waves, and the turmoil of the nations. They also who dwell in faraway places are afraid at your wonders. You call the morning's dawn and the evening with songs of joy. You visit the earth, and water it.

You greatly enrich it. The river of God is full of water. You provide them grain, for so you have ordained it. You drench its furrows. You level its ridges. You soften it with showers. You bless it with a crop. You crown the year with your bounty. Your carts overflow with abundance.

The wilderness grasslands overflow. The hills are clothed with gladness. The pastures are covered with flocks. The valleys also are clothed with grain. They shout for joy. They also sing.

PSALM 65

CHAPTER 25

Make a joyful shout to God, all the earth. Sing to the glory of his name. Offer glory and praise. Tell God, "How awesome are your deeds. Through the greatness of your power, your enemies submit themselves to you.

All the earth will worship you, and will sing to you; they will sing to your name." Selah. Come, and see God's deeds — awesome work on behalf of the children of men.

He turned the sea into dry land. They went through the river on foot. There, we rejoiced in him. He rules by his might forever. His eyes watch the nations. Do not let the rebellious rise up against him. Selah. Praise our God, you peoples.

Make the sound of his praise heard, who preserves our life among the living, and doesn't allow our feet to be moved. For you, God, have tested us. You have refined us, as silver is refined. You brought us into prison. You laid a burden on our backs.

You allowed men to ride over our heads. We went through fire and through water, but you brought us to the place of abundance. I will come into your temple with burnt offerings. I will pay my vows to you, which my lips promised, and my mouth spoke, when I was in distress.

I will offer to you burnt offerings of fat animals, with the offering of rams, I will offer bulls with goats. Selah. Come, and hear, all you who fear God. I will declare what he has done for my soul. I cried to him with my mouth. He was extolled with my tongue.

If I cherished sin in my heart, the Lord wouldn't have listened. But most certainly, God has listened. He has heard the voice of my prayer. Blessed be God, who has not turned away my prayer, nor his loving kindness from me.

PSALM 66

CHAPTER 26

May God be merciful to us, bless us, and cause his face to shine on us. Selah. That your way may be known on earth, and your salvation among all nations, let the peoples praise you, God.

Let all the peoples praise you. Let the nations be glad and sing for joy, for you will judge the world in righteousness. You will judge the peoples with equity, and guide the nations on earth. Let the peoples praise you, God. Let all the peoples praise you. The earth has yielded its increase.

God, even our own God, will bless us. God will bless us. Every part of the earth shall fear him.

PSALM 67

CHAPTER 27

God, give the king your justice; your righteousness to the royal son. He will judge your people with righteousness, and your poor with justice. The mountains shall bring prosperity to the people. The hills bring the fruit of righteousness.

He will judge the poor of the people. He will save the children of the needy, and will break the oppressor in pieces. They shall fear you while the sun endures; and as long as the moon, throughout all generations. He will come down like rain on the mown grass, as showers that water the earth.

In his days, the righteous shall flourish, and abundance of peace, until the moon is no more. He shall have dominion also from sea to sea, from the River to the farthest parts of the earth. Those who dwell in the wilderness shall bow before him. His enemies shall lick the dust.

The kings of Tarshish and of the islands will bring tribute. The kings of Sheba and Seba shall offer gifts. Yes, all kings shall fall down before him. All nations shall serve him.

For he will deliver the needy when he cries; the poor, who has no helper. He will have pity on the poor and needy. He will save the souls of the needy.

He will redeem their soul from oppression and violence. Their blood will be precious in his sight. And he shall live, and the gold of Sheba shall be given to him. Men shall pray for him continually. He shall bless him all day long.

There shall be abundance of grain throughout the land. Its fruit sways like Lebanon. Let it flourish, thriving like the grass of the field. His name endures forever. His name continues as long as the sun.

Men shall be blessed by him. All nations will call him blessed. Praise be to the LORD, the God of Israel, who alone does marvelous deeds. Blessed be his glorious name forever. Let the whole earth be filled with his glory. Amen and amen. This ends the prayers by David, the son of Jesse.

PSALM 72

CHAPTER 28

We give thanks to you, God. We give thanks, for your Name is near. Men tell about your wondrous works. When I choose the appointed time, I will judge blamelessly. The earth and all its inhabitants quake.

I firmly hold its pillars. Selah. I said to the arrogant, "Do not boast." I said to the wicked, "Do not lift up the horn. Do not lift up your horn on high. Do not speak with a stiff neck." For neither from the east, nor from the west, nor yet from the south, comes exaltation.

But God is the judge. He puts down one, and lifts up another. For in the hand of the LORD there is a cup, full of foaming wine mixed with spices. He pours it out. Indeed the wicked of the earth drink and drink it to its very dregs.

But I will declare this forever: I will sing praises to the God of Jacob. I will cut off all the horns of the wicked, but the horns of the righteous shall be lifted up.

PSALM 75

CHAPTER 29

I will sing of the loving kindness of the LORD forever. With my mouth I will make known your faithfulness to all generations. I indeed declare, "Love stands firm forever. You established the heavens. Your faithfulness is in them." "I have made a covenant with my chosen one, I have sworn to David, my servant, 'I will establish your offspring forever, and build up your throne for all generations.'" Selah.

The heavens will praise your wonders, LORD; your faithfulness also in the assembly of the holy ones. For who in the skies can be compared to the LORD? Who among the sons of God is like the LORD, a very awesome God in the council of the holy ones, to be feared above all those who are around him?

LORD, God of hosts, who is a mighty one like you, LORD? Your faithfulness is around you. You rule the pride of the sea.

When its waves rise up, you calm them. You have broken Rahab in pieces, like one of the slain. You have scattered your enemies with your mighty arm. The heavens are yours. The earth also is yours; the world and its fullness. You have founded them. The north and the south, you have created them. Tabor and Hermon rejoice in your name.

You have a mighty arm. Your hand is strong, and your right hand is exalted. Righteousness and justice are the foundation of your throne. Loving kindness and truth go before your face.

Blessed are the people who know the joyful shout. They walk in the light of your presence, LORD. In your name they rejoice all day. In your righteousness, they are exalted.

For you are the glory of their strength. In your favor, our horn will be exalted. For our shield belongs to the LORD; our king to the Holy One of Israel. Then you spoke in a vision to your faithful ones, and said, "I have bestowed strength on the warrior.

I have exalted a young man from the people. I have found David, my servant. I have anointed him with my holy oil, with whom my hand shall be established. My arm will also strengthen him.

No enemy will tax him. No wicked man will oppress him. I will beat down his adversaries before him, and strike those who hate him.

But my faithfulness and my loving kindness will be with him. In my name, his horn will be exalted. I will set his hand also on the sea, and his right hand on the rivers. He will call to me, 'You are my Father, my God, and the rock of my salvation.'

I will also appoint him my firstborn, the highest of the kings of the earth. I will keep my loving kindness for him forevermore.

My covenant will stand firm with him. And I will establish his descendants forever, and his throne as the days of heaven. If his children forsake my Law, and do not walk in my ordinances; if they break my statutes, and do not keep my commandments; then I will punish their sin with the rod, and their iniquity with stripes.

But I will not completely take my loving kindness from him, nor allow my faithfulness to fail.

I will not break my covenant, nor alter what my lips have uttered. Once have I sworn by my holiness, I will not lie to David. His descendants will endure forever, his throne like the sun before me.

It will be established forever like the moon, the faithful witness in the sky." Selah. But you have rejected and spurned.

You have been angry with your anointed. You have renounced the covenant of your servant. You have defiled his crown in the dust. You have broken down all his hedges. You have brought his strongholds to ruin.

All who pass by the way rob him. He has become a reproach to his neighbors. You have exalted the right hand of his adversaries.

You have made all of his enemies rejoice. Yes, you turn back the edge of his sword, and haven't supported him in battle. You have ended his splendor, and thrown his throne down to the ground.

You have shortened the days of his youth. You have covered him with shame. Selah. How long, LORD? Will you hide yourself forever?

Will your wrath burn like fire? Remember how short my time is. For what vanity have you created all the children of men. What man is he who shall live and not see death, who shall deliver his soul from the power of Sheol? Selah.

Lord, where are your former loving kindnesses, which you swore to David in your faithfulness?

Remember, Lord, the reproach of your servants, how I bear in my heart the taunts of all the mighty peoples, with which your enemies have mocked, LORD, with which they have mocked the footsteps of your anointed one.

Blessed be the LORD forevermore. Amen, and Amen.

PSALM 89

CHAPTER 30

It is a good thing to give thanks to the LORD, to sing praises to your name, Most High; to proclaim your loving kindness in the morning, and your faithfulness every night, with the ten-stringed lute, with the harp, and with the melody of the lyre. For you, LORD, have made me glad through your work.

I will triumph in the works of your hands. How great are your works, LORD. Your thoughts are very deep. A senseless man doesn't know, neither does a fool understand this: though the wicked spring up as the grass, and all the evildoers flourish, they will be destroyed forever. But you, LORD, are on high forevermore.

For, look, your enemies, LORD, for, look, your enemies shall perish. All the evildoers will be scattered. But you have exalted my horn like that of the wild ox. I am anointed with fresh oil. My eye has also seen my enemies. My ears have heard of the wicked enemies who rise up against me.

The righteous shall flourish like the palm tree. He will grow like a cedar in Lebanon. They are planted in the LORD's house. They will flourish in our God's courts.

They will still bring forth fruit in old age. They will be full of sap and green, to show that the LORD is upright. He is my Rock, and there is no unrighteousness in him.

PSALM 92

CHAPTER 31

I will sing of loving kindness and justice. To you, LORD, I will sing praises. I will be careful to live a blameless life. When will you come to me? I will walk within my house with a blameless heart. I will set no vile thing before my eyes. I hate the deeds of faithless men. They will not cling to me. A perverse heart will be far from me.

I will have nothing to do with evil. I will silence whoever secretly slanders his neighbor. I won't tolerate one who is haughty and conceited. My eyes will be on the faithful of the land, that they may dwell with me.

He who walks in a perfect way, he will serve me. He who practices deceit won't dwell within my house.

He who speaks falsehood won't be established before my eyes. Morning by morning, I will destroy all the wicked of the land; to cut off all evildoers from the LORD's city.

PSALM 101

CHAPTER 32

Give thanks to the LORD. Call on his name. Make his deeds known among the peoples. Sing to him, sing praises to him. Tell of all his marvelous works. Glory in his holy name. Let the heart of those who seek the LORD rejoice.

Seek the LORD and his strength. Seek his face forever more. Remember his marvelous works that he has done; his wonders, and the judgments of his mouth, you offspring of Abraham, his servant, you children of Jacob, his chosen ones.

He is the LORD, our God. His judgments are in all the earth. He has remembered his covenant forever, the word which he commanded to a thousand generations, the covenant which he made with Abraham, his oath to Isaac, and confirmed the same to Jacob for a statute; to Israel for an everlasting covenant, saying,

"To you I will give the land of Canaan, the lot of your inheritance;" when they were but a few men in number, yes, very few, and foreigners in it.

They went about from nation to nation, from one kingdom to another people. He allowed no one to do them wrong. Yes, he reproved kings for their sakes, "Do not touch my anointed ones. Do my prophets no harm." He called for a famine on the land. He destroyed the food supplies. He sent a man before them.

Joseph was sold for a slave. They bruised his feet with shackles. His neck was locked in irons, until the time that his word happened, and the LORD's word proved him true.

The king sent and freed him; even the ruler of peoples, and let him go free. He made him lord of his house, and ruler of all of his possessions; to discipline his princes at his pleasure, and to teach his elders wisdom.

Israel also came into Egypt. Jacob sojourned in the land of Ham. He increased his people greatly, and made them stronger than their adversaries. He turned their heart to hate his people, to conspire against his servants. He sent Moses, his servant, and Aaron, whom he had chosen.

They performed miracles among them, and wonders in the land of Ham. He sent darkness, and made it dark. They did not rebel against his words. He turned their waters into blood, and killed their fish. Their land swarmed with frogs, even in the chambers of their kings. He spoke, and swarms of flies came, and gnats in all their territory.

He gave them hail for rain, flaming fire in their land. He struck their vines and also their fig trees, and shattered the trees of their country.

He spoke, and the locusts came, and the grasshoppers, without number, ate up every plant in their land; and ate up the fruit of their ground. He struck also all the firstborn in their land, the first fruits of all their manhood.

And he brought them out with silver and gold, and there was no one among their tribes who stumbled. Egypt was glad when they departed, for the fear of them had fallen on them.

He spread a cloud for a covering, fire to give light in the night. They asked, and he brought quails, and satisfied them with the bread of the sky. He opened the rock, and waters gushed out.

They ran as a river in the dry places. For he remembered his holy word, and Abraham, his servant. He brought forth his people with joy, his chosen with singing.

He gave them the lands of the nations. They took the labor of the peoples in possession, that they might keep his statutes, and observe his laws. Praise the LORD.

PSALM 105

CHAPTER 33

Praise the LORD. Give thanks to the LORD, for he is good, for his loving kindness endures forever. Who can utter the mighty acts of the LORD, or fully declare all his praise?

Blessed are those who uphold justice, who practice righteousness at all times. Remember me, LORD, with the favor that you show to your people.

Visit me with your salvation, that I may see the prosperity of your chosen, that I may rejoice in the gladness of your nation, that I may glory with your inheritance. We have sinned with our fathers. We have committed iniquity. We have done wickedly. Our fathers did not understand your wonders in Egypt.

They did not remember the multitude of your loving kindnesses, but were rebellious at the sea, even at the Sea of Suf. Nevertheless he saved them for his name's sake, that he might make his mighty power known.

He rebuked the Sea of Suf also, and it was dried up; so he led them through the depths, as through a desert. He saved them from the hand of him who hated them, and redeemed them from the hand of the enemy.

The waters covered their adversaries. There was not one of them left. Then they believed his words. They sang his praise. They soon forgot his works.

They did not wait for his counsel, but gave in to craving in the desert, and tested God in the wasteland. He gave them their request, but sent leanness into their soul. They envied Moses also in the camp, and Aaron, the LORD's holy one.

The earth opened and swallowed up Dathan, and covered the company of Abiram. A fire was kindled in their company. The flame burned up the wicked. They made a calf in Horeb, and worshiped a molten image.

Thus they exchanged their glory for an image of a bull that eats grass. They forgot God, their Savior, who had done great things in Egypt, Wondrous works in the land of Ham, and awesome things by the Sea of Suf.

Therefore he said that he would destroy them, had Moses, his chosen, not stood before him in the breach, to turn away his wrath, so that he wouldn't destroy them. Yes, they despised the pleasant land.

They did not believe his word, but murmured in their tents, and did not listen to the LORD's voice. Therefore he swore to them that he would overthrow them in the wilderness, and that he would make their offspring fall among the nations, and scatter them in the lands.

They joined themselves also to Baal Peor, and ate the sacrifices of the dead. Thus they provoked him to anger with their deeds. The plague broke in on them. Then Phinehas stood up, and executed judgment, so the plague was stopped.

That was credited to him for righteousness, for all generations to come. They angered him also at the waters of Meribah, so that Moses was troubled for their sakes; because they were rebellious against his spirit, he spoke rashly with his lips.

They did not destroy the peoples, as the LORD commanded them, but mixed themselves with the nations, and learned their works. They served their idols, which became a snare to them.

Yes, they sacrificed their sons and their daughters to demons. They shed innocent blood, even the blood of their sons and of their daughters, whom they sacrificed to the idols of Canaan.

The land was polluted with blood. Thus were they defiled with their works, and prostituted themselves in their deeds. Therefore the LORD burned with anger against his people.

He abhorred his inheritance. He gave them into the hand of the nations. Those who hated them ruled over them. Their enemies also oppressed them. They were brought into subjection under their hand.

Many times he delivered them, but they were rebellious in their counsel, and were brought low in their iniquity. Nevertheless he regarded their distress, when he heard their cry. He remembered for them his covenant, and repented according to the multitude of his loving kindnesses.

He made them also to be pitied by all those who carried them captive. Save us, LORD, our God, gather us from among the nations, to give thanks to your holy name, to triumph in your praise.

Blessed be the LORD, the God of Israel, from everlasting to everlasting. And let all the people say, "Amen." Praise the LORD.

PSALM 106

CHAPTER 34

Give thanks to the LORD, for he is good, for his loving kindness endures forever. Let the redeemed by the LORD say so, whom he has redeemed from the hand of the adversary, and gathered out of the lands, from the east and from the west, from the north and from the south.

They wandered in the wilderness in a desert way. They found no city to live in. Hungry and thirsty, their soul fainted in them.

Then they cried to the LORD in their trouble, and he delivered them out of their distresses, he led them also by a straight way, that they might go to a city to live in. Let them praise the LORD for his loving kindness, for his wonderful works to the children of men.

For he satisfies the longing soul. He fills the hungry soul with good. Some sat in darkness and in the shadow of death, being bound in affliction and iron, because they rebelled against the words of God, and condemned the counsel of the Most High. Therefore he brought down their heart with labor. They fell down, and there was none to help.

Then they cried to the LORD in their trouble, and he saved them out of their distresses. He brought them out of darkness and the shadow of death, and broke their bonds in sunder. Let them praise the LORD for his loving kindness, for his wonderful works to the children of men.

For he has broken the gates of bronze, and cut through bars of iron. Fools are afflicted because of their disobedience, and because of their iniquities.

Their soul abhors all kinds of food. They draw near to the gates of death. Then they cry to the LORD in their trouble, he saves them out of their distresses. He sent his word and healed them, and delivered them from the pit. Let them praise the LORD for his loving kindness, for his wonderful works to the children of men.

Let them offer the sacrifices of thanksgiving, and declare his works with singing. Those who go down to the sea in ships, who do business in great waters; these see the LORD's works, and his wonders in the deep.

For he commands, and raises the stormy wind, which lifts up its waves. They mount up to the sky; they go down again to the depths. Their soul melts away because of trouble.

They reel back and forth, and stagger like a drunken man, and are at their wits' end. Then they cry to the LORD in their trouble, and he brings them out of their distress. He makes the storm a calm, so that its waves are still.

Then they are glad because it is calm, so he brings them to their desired haven. Let them praise the LORD for his loving kindness, for his wonderful works for the children of men.

Let them exalt him also in the assembly of the people, and praise him in the seat of the elders. He turns rivers into a desert, water springs into a thirsty ground, and a fruitful land into a salt waste, for the wickedness of those who dwell in it. He turns a desert into a pool of water, and a dry land into water springs.

There he makes the hungry live, that they may prepare a city to live in, sow fields, plant vineyards, and reap the fruits of increase. He blesses them also, so that they are multiplied greatly. He doesn't allow their livestock to decrease. Again, they are diminished and bowed down through oppression, trouble, and sorrow.

He pours contempt on princes, and causes them to wander in a trackless waste. Yet he lifts the needy out of their affliction, and increases their families like a flock. The upright will see it, and be glad. All the wicked will shut their mouths.

Whoever is wise will pay attention to these things. They will consider the loving kindnesses of the LORD.

PSALM 107

CHAPTER 35

The LORD says to my Lord, "Sit at my right hand, until I make your enemies your footstool for your feet." The LORD will send forth the rod of your strength out of Zion. Rule in the midst of your enemies. Your people offer themselves willingly in the day of your power, in holy array.

Out of the womb of the morning, you have the dew of your youth. The LORD has sworn, and will not change his mind: "You are a priest forever in the order of Melchizedek."

The Lord is at your right hand. He will crush kings in the day of his wrath. He will judge among the nations. He will heap up dead bodies. He will crush the ruler of the whole earth.

He will drink of the brook in the way; therefore he will lift up his head.

PSALM 110

CHAPTER 36

I love the LORD, because he listens to my voice, and my cries for mercy. Because he has turned his ear to me, therefore I will call on him as long as I live. The cords of death surrounded me, the pains of Sheol got a hold of me.

I found trouble and sorrow. Then I called on the name of the LORD: "LORD, I beg you, deliver my soul."

The LORD is Gracious and righteous. Yes, our God is merciful. The LORD preserves the simple. I was brought low, and he saved me. Return to your rest, my soul, for the LORD has dealt bountifully with you.

For you have delivered my soul from death, my eyes from tears, and my feet from falling.

I will walk before the LORD in the land of the living. I believed, therefore I said, "I am greatly afflicted." I said in my haste, "All men are liars."

What will I give to the LORD for all his benefits toward me? I will take the cup of salvation, and call on the name of the LORD.

I will pay my vows to the LORD, yes, in the presence of all his people. Precious in the sight of the LORD is the death of his faithful ones. LORD, truly I am your servant.

I am your servant, the son of your handmaid. You have freed me from my chains. I will offer to you the sacrifice of thanksgiving, and will call on the name of the LORD.

I will pay my vows to the LORD, yes, in the presence of all his people, in the courts of the LORD's house, in the midst of you, Jerusalem. Praise the LORD.

PSALM 116

CHAPTER 37

Give thanks to the LORD, for he is good, for his loving kindness endures forever. Let Israel now say that his loving kindness endures forever. Let the house of Aaron now say that his loving kindness endures forever. Now let those who fear the LORD say that his loving kindness endures forever.

Out of my distress, I called on the LORD. The LORD answered me with freedom. The LORD is my helper; I will not fear. What can man do to me? The LORD is my helper; and I will look in triumph on those who hate me. It is better to take refuge in the LORD, than to put confidence in man.

It is better to take refuge in the LORD, than to put confidence in princes. All the nations surrounded me, but in the name of the LORD, I cut them off. They surrounded me, yes, they surrounded me.

In the name of the LORD I indeed cut them off. They surrounded me like bees. They are quenched like the burning thorns. In the name of the LORD I cut them off.

You pushed me back hard, to make me fall, but the LORD helped me. The LORD is my strength and song. He has become my salvation. The voice of rejoicing and salvation is in the tents of the righteous. "

The right hand of the LORD does valiantly. The right hand of the LORD is exalted. The right hand of the LORD does valiantly." I will not die, but live, and declare the works of the LORD.

The LORD has punished me severely, but he has not given me over to death. Open to me the gates of righteousness. I will enter into them and praise the LORD. This is the gate of the LORD; the righteous will enter into it.

I will give thanks to you, for you have answered me, and have become my salvation. The stone which the builders rejected has become the cornerstone.

This is the LORD's doing. It is marvelous in our eyes. This is the day that the LORD has made. We will rejoice and be glad in it. Save us now, we beg you, LORD. LORD, we beg you, send prosperity now. Blessed is he who comes in the name of the LORD. We have blessed you out of the house of the LORD.

The LORD is God, and he has given us light. Bind the sacrifice with cords, even to the horns of the altar. You are my God, and I will give thanks to you. You are my God, I will exalt you. Oh give thanks to the LORD, for he is good, for his loving kindness endures forever.

PSALM 118

CHAPTER 38

In my distress, I cried to the LORD. He answered me. Deliver my soul, LORD, from lying lips, from a deceitful tongue. What will be given to you, and what will be done more to you, you deceitful tongue?

Sharp arrows of the mighty, with coals of juniper. Woe is me, that I live in Meshech, that I dwell among the tents of Kedar. My soul has had her dwelling too long with him who hates peace. I am for peace, but when I speak, they are for war.

PSALM 120

CHAPTER 39

If it had not been the LORD who was on our side, let Israel now say, if it had not been the LORD who was on our side, when men rose up against us; then they would have swallowed us up alive, when their wrath was kindled against us; then the waters would have overwhelmed us, the stream would have gone over our soul; then the proud waters would have gone over our soul.

Blessed be the LORD, who has not given us as a prey to their teeth. Our soul has escaped like a bird out of the fowler's snare. The snare is broken, and we have escaped. Our help is in the name of the LORD, who made heaven and earth.

PSALM 124

CHAPTER 40

Many times they have afflicted me from my youth up. Let Israel now say, many times they have afflicted me from my youth up, yet they have not prevailed against me. The plowers plowed on my back. They made their furrows long.

The LORD is righteous. He has cut apart the cords of the wicked. Let them be disappointed and turned backward, all those who hate Zion.

Let them be as the grass on the housetops, which withers before it grows up; with which the reaper doesn't fill his hand, nor he who binds sheaves, his bosom. Neither do those who go by say, "The blessing of the LORD be on you. We bless you in the name of the LORD."

PSALM 129

CHAPTER 41

LORD, remember David and all his affliction, how he swore to the LORD, and vowed to the Mighty One of Jacob: "Surely I will not come into the structure of my house, nor go up into my bed;

I will not give sleep to my eyes, or slumber to my eyelids; until I find out a place for the LORD, a dwelling for the Mighty One of Jacob."

Look, we heard of it in Ephrathah. We found it in the field of Jaar: "We will go into his dwelling place. We will worship at his footstool. Arise, LORD, to your resting place, you and the ark of your strength. Let your priest be clothed with righteousness. Let your faithful ones shout for joy."

For your servant David's sake, do not turn away the face of your anointed one. The LORD has sworn to David in truth. He will not turn from it:

"I will set the fruit of your body on your throne. If your children will keep my covenant, my testimony that I will teach them, their children also will sit on your throne forevermore."

For the LORD has chosen Zion; he has desired it for his dwelling. "This is my resting place forever. Here I will live, for I have desired it. I will abundantly bless her provision. I will satisfy her poor with bread.

Her priests I will also clothe with salvation. Her faithful ones will shout aloud for joy. There I will make the horn of David to bud.

I have ordained a lamp for my anointed. I will clothe his enemies with shame, but on himself, his crown will be resplendent."

PSALM 132

CHAPTER 42

Give thanks to the LORD, for he is good; for his loving kindness endures forever. Give thanks to the God of gods; for his loving kindness endures forever.

Give thanks to the Lord of lords; for his loving kindness endures forever: To him who alone does great wonders; for his loving kindness endures forever: To him who by understanding made the heavens; for his loving kindness endures forever: To him who spread out the earth above the waters; for his loving kindness endures forever: To him who made the great lights; for his loving kindness endures forever: The sun to rule by day; for his loving kindness endures forever; The moon and stars to rule by night; for his loving kindness endures forever: To him who struck down the Egyptian firstborn; for his loving kindness endures forever;

And brought out Israel from among them; for his loving kindness endures forever; With a strong hand, and with an outstretched arm; for his loving kindness endures forever: To him who divided the Sea of Suf apart; for his loving kindness endures forever; And made Israel to pass through its midst; for his loving kindness endures forever; But overthrew Pharaoh and his army in the Sea of Suf; for his loving kindness endures forever: To him who led his people through the wilderness; for his loving kindness endures forever: To him who struck great kings; for his loving kindness endures forever;

And killed mighty kings; for his loving kindness endures forever: Sihon king of the Amorites; for his loving kindness endures forever; Og king of Bashan; for his loving kindness endures forever; And gave their land as an inheritance; for his loving kindness endures forever;

Even a heritage to Israel his servant; for his loving kindness endures forever: Who remembered us in our low estate; for his loving kindness endures forever; and has delivered us from our adversaries; for his loving kindness endures forever: Who gives food to every creature; for his loving kindness endures forever.

Oh give thanks to the God of heaven; for his loving kindness endures forever.

PSALM 136

CHAPTER 43

I will give you thanks with my whole heart. Before the angels, I will sing praises to you. I will bow down toward your holy temple, and give thanks to your Name for your loving kindness and for your truth; for you have exalted your Name and your word above all.

In the day that I called, you answered me. You encouraged me with strength in my soul. All the kings of the earth will give you thanks, LORD, for they have heard the words of your mouth. Yes, they will sing of the ways of the LORD; for great is the LORD's glory.

For though the LORD is high, yet he looks after the lowly; but the proud, he knows from afar. Though I walk in the midst of trouble, you will revive me. You will stretch forth your hand against the wrath of my enemies.

Your right hand will save me. The LORD will fulfill that which concerns me; your loving kindness, LORD, endures forever. Do not forsake the works of your own hands.

PSALM 138

CHAPTER 44

Blessed be the LORD, my Rock, who teaches my hands to war, and my fingers to battle: my loving kindness, my fortress, my high tower, my deliverer, my shield, and he in whom I take refuge; who subdues peoples under me. LORD, what is man, that you care for him? Or the son of man, that you think of him?

Man is like a breath. His days are like a shadow that passes away. Part your heavens, LORD, and come down. Touch the mountains, and they will smoke. Throw out lightning, and scatter them.

Send out your arrows, and rout them. Stretch out your hand from above, rescue me, and deliver me out of great waters, out of the hands of foreigners; whose mouths speak deceit, whose right hand is a right hand of falsehood.

I will sing a new song to you, God. On a ten-stringed lyre, I will sing praises to you. You are he who gives salvation to kings, who rescues David, his servant, from the deadly sword.

Rescue me, and deliver me out of the hands of foreigners, whose mouths speak deceit, whose right hand is a right hand of falsehood.

Then our sons will be like well-nurtured plants, our daughters like pillars carved to adorn a palace. Our storehouses are full, filled with all kinds of provision. Our sheep bring forth thousands and ten thousands in our fields. Our oxen will pull heavy loads.

There is no breaking in, and no going away, and no outcry in our streets. Blessed are the people who are in such a situation. Blessed are the people whose God is the LORD.

PSALM 144

SONGS & PRAYERS OF TRUST

CHAPTER 45

In the LORD, I take refuge. How can you say to my soul, "Flee as a bird to your mountain." For, look, the wicked bend their bows. They set their arrows on the strings, that they may shoot in darkness at the upright in heart.

If the foundations are destroyed, what can the righteous do? The LORD is in his holy temple. The LORD is on his throne in heaven. His eyes look upon the poor. His eyes examine the children of men. The LORD examines the righteous, but the wicked and the one who loves violence his soul hates.

On the wicked he will rain blazing coals; fire, sulfur, and scorching wind shall be the portion of their cup. For the LORD is righteous. He loves righteousness. The upright shall see his face.

PSALM 11

CHAPTER 46

Preserve me, God, for in you do I take refuge. I said to the LORD, "You are my Lord. Apart from you I have no good thing." As for the holy ones who are in the land, they are the excellent ones in whom is all my delight.

Their sorrows will multiply who pay a dowry for another (god). Their drink offerings of blood I will not offer, nor take their names on my lips. The LORD is the portion of my inheritance and my cup. You made my lot secure.

The lines have fallen to me in pleasant places. Yes, beautiful is my inheritance. I will bless the LORD, who has given me counsel. Yes, my heart instructs me in the night seasons. I have set the LORD always before me; because he is at my right hand, I will not be shaken.

Therefore my heart is glad, and my tongue rejoices. My body shall also dwell in safety. For you will not abandon my soul in Sheol, neither will you allow your Holy One to see decay. You make known to me the path of life.

In your presence is fullness of joy. In your right hand there are pleasures forevermore.

PSALM 16

CHAPTER 47

The LORD is my shepherd; I lack nothing. He makes me lie down in green pastures. He leads me beside still waters. He restores my soul.

He guides me in the paths of righteousness for his name's sake. Even though I walk through the valley of the shadow of death, I will fear no evil, for you are with me.

Your rod and your staff, they comfort me. You prepare a table before me in the presence of my enemies. You anoint my head with oil. My cup runs over.

Surely goodness and loving kindness shall follow me all the days of my life, and I will dwell in the LORD's house forever.

PSALM 23

CHAPTER 48

The LORD is my light and my salvation. Whom shall I fear? The LORD is the stronghold of my life. Of whom shall I be afraid? When evildoers came at me to eat up my flesh, even my adversaries and my foes, they stumbled and fell.

Though an army is deployed against me, my heart shall not fear. Though war should rise against me, even then I will be confident. One thing I have asked of the LORD, that I will seek after, that I may dwell in the house of the LORD all the days of my life, to see the LORD's beauty, and to inquire in his temple.

For in the day of trouble he will keep me secretly in his pavilion. In the covert of his tabernacle he will hide me. He will lift me up on a rock. Now my head will be lifted up above my enemies around me.

I will offer sacrifices of joy in his tent. I will sing, yes, I will sing praises to the LORD. Hear, LORD, when I cry with my voice. Have mercy also on me, and answer me. When you said, "Seek my face," my heart said to you, "I will seek your face, LORD."

Do not hide your face from me. Do not put your servant away in anger. You have been my help. Do not abandon me, neither forsake me, God of my salvation. When my father and my mother forsake me, then the LORD will take me up. Teach me your way, LORD.

Lead me in a straight path, because of my enemies. Do not deliver me over to the desire of my adversaries, for false witnesses have risen up against me, such as breathe out violence. I am still confident of this: I will see the goodness of the LORD in the land of the living.

Wait for the LORD. Be strong, and let your heart take courage. Yes, wait for the LORD.

PSALM 27

CHAPTER 49

In you, LORD, I take refuge. Let me never be disappointed. Deliver me in your righteousness. Bow down your ear to me. Deliver me speedily. Be to me a strong rock, a house of defense to save me.

For you are my rock and my fortress, therefore for your name's sake lead me and guide me. Pluck me out of the net that they have laid secretly for me, for you are my stronghold. Into your hands I commit my spirit.

You redeem me, LORD, God of truth. I hate those who regard lying vanities, but I trust in the LORD. I will be glad and rejoice in your loving kindness, for you have seen my affliction. You have known my soul in adversities. You have not shut me up into the hand of the enemy.

You have set my feet in a large place. Have mercy on me, LORD, for I am in distress. My eye, my soul, and my body waste away with grief. For my life is spent with sorrow, my years with sighing. My strength fails because of my affliction, and my bones waste away.

Because of all my adversaries I have become utterly contemptible to my neighbors, a fear to my acquaintances. Those who saw me on the street fled from me. I am forgotten from their hearts like a dead man. I am like broken pottery.

For I have heard the slander of many, terror on every side, while they conspire together against me, they plot to take away my life. But I trust in you, LORD. I said, "You are my God."

My times are in your hand. Deliver me from the hand of my enemies, and from those who persecute me. Make your face to shine on your servant. Save me in your loving kindness. Let me not be disappointed, LORD, for I have called on you.

Let the wicked be disappointed. Let them be silent in Sheol. Let the lying lips be mute, which speak against the righteous insolently, with pride and contempt. Oh how great is your goodness, which you have stored up for those who fear you, which you have worked for those who take refuge in you, before the sons of men.

In the shelter of your presence you will hide them from the plotting of man. You will keep them secretly in a dwelling away from the strife of tongues. Praise be to the LORD, for he has shown me his marvelous loving kindness in a besieged city.

As for me, I said in my haste, "I am cut off from before your eyes." Nevertheless you heard the voice of my petitions when I cried to you. Oh love the LORD, all you his faithful ones.

The LORD preserves the faithful, and fully recompenses him who behaves arrogantly. Be strong, and let your heart take courage, all you who hope in the LORD.

PSALM 31

CHAPTER 50

Save me, God, by your name. Vindicate me in your might. Hear my prayer, God. Listen to the words of my mouth. For strangers have risen up against me. Violent men have sought after my soul. They haven't set God before them. Selah.

Look, God is my helper. The Lord is the one who sustains my soul. He will repay the evil to my enemies. Destroy them in your truth. With a free will offering, I will sacrifice to you. I will give thanks to your name, LORD, for it is good.

For he has delivered me out of all trouble. My eye has seen triumph over my enemies.

PSALM 54

CHAPTER 51

Be merciful to me, God, for man wants to swallow me up. All day long, he attacks and oppresses me. My enemies want to swallow me up all day long, for they are many who fight proudly against me.

When I am afraid, I will put my trust in you. In God, I praise his word. In God, I put my trust. I will not be afraid. What can flesh do to me? All day long they twist my words. All their thoughts are against me for evil.

They conspire and lurk, watching my steps, they are eager to take my life. Shall they escape by iniquity? In anger cast down the peoples, God. You number my wanderings. You put my tears into your bottle.

Aren't they in your book? Then my enemies shall turn back in the day that I call. I know this, that God is for me. In God, I will praise his word. In the LORD, I will praise his word.

I have put my trust in God. I will not be afraid. What can man do to me? Your vows are on me, God. I will give thank offerings to you.

For you have delivered my soul from death, and prevented my feet from falling, that I may walk before God in the light of the living.

PSALM 56

CHAPTER 52

My soul rests in God alone, for my salvation is from him. He alone is my rock and my salvation, my fortress – I will never be greatly shaken. How long will you assault a man, would all of you throw him down, like a leaning wall, like a tottering fence? They fully intend to throw him down from his lofty place. They delight in lies.

They bless with their mouth, but they curse inwardly. Selah. My soul, wait in silence for God alone, for my expectation is from him. He alone is my rock and my salvation, my fortress. I will not be shaken.

With God is my salvation and my honor. The rock of my strength, and my refuge, is in God. Trust in him at all times, O people. Pour out your heart before him. God is a refuge for us. Selah.

Surely men of low degree are just a breath, and men of high degree are a lie. In the balances they will go up. They are together lighter than a breath. Do not trust in oppression. Do not become vain in robbery.

If riches increase, do not set your heart on them. God has spoken once; twice I have heard this, that power belongs to God. Also to you, Lord, belongs loving kindness, for you reward every man according to his work.

PSALM 62

CHAPTER 53

God, you are my God. I will earnestly seek you. My soul thirsts for you. My flesh longs for you, in a dry and weary land, where there is no water.

So I have seen you in the sanctuary, watching your power and your glory. Because your loving kindness is better than life, my lips shall praise you. So I will bless you while I live. I will lift up my hands in your name.

My soul shall be satisfied as with the richest food. My mouth shall praise you with joyful lips, when I remember you on my bed, and think about you in the night watches. For you have been my help.

I will rejoice in the shadow of your wings. My soul stays close to you. Your right hand holds me up. But those who seek my soul, to destroy it, shall go into the lower parts of the earth.

They shall be given over to the power of the sword. They shall be jackal food. But the king shall rejoice in God.

Everyone who swears by him will praise him, for the mouth of those who speak lies shall be silenced.

PSALM 63

CHAPTER 54

He who dwells in the secret place of the Most High will rest in the shadow of Shaddai. I will say of the LORD, "He is my refuge and my fortress; my God, in whom I trust."

For he will deliver you from the snare of the fowler, and from the deadly pestilence. He will cover you with his feathers. Under his wings you will take refuge. His faithfulness is a shield and a wall.

You shall not be afraid of the terror by night, nor of the arrow that flies by day; nor of the pestilence that walks in darkness, nor of the destruction that wastes at noonday. A thousand may fall at your side, and ten thousand at your right hand; but it will not come near you.

You will only look with your eyes, and see the recompense of the wicked. Because you have made the LORD your refuge, and the Most High your dwelling place, no evil shall overtake you; no plague shall come near your dwelling.

For he will put his angels in charge of you, to guard you in all your ways. In their hands they will lift you up, so that you will not strike your foot against a stone. You will tread upon the lion and the viper.

You will trample the young lion and the serpent underfoot. "Because he has set his love on me, therefore I will deliver him. I will set him on high, because he has known my name.

He will call on me, and I will answer him. I will be with him in trouble. I will deliver him, and honor him. I will satisfy him with long life, and show him my salvation."

PSALM 91

CHAPTER 55

I will lift up my eyes to the hills. Where does my help come from? My help comes from the LORD, who made heaven and earth. He will not allow your foot to be moved. He who keeps you will not slumber.

Look, he who keeps Israel will neither slumber nor sleep. The LORD is your keeper. The LORD is your shade on your right hand. The sun will not harm you by day, nor the moon by night.

The LORD will keep you from all evil. He will keep your soul. The LORD will keep your going out and your coming in, from this time forth, and forevermore.

PSALM 121

CHAPTER 56

Those who trust in the LORD are as Mount Zion, which cannot be moved, but remains forever. As the mountains surround Jerusalem, so the LORD surrounds his people from this time forth and forevermore.

For the scepter of wickedness won't remain over the allotment of the righteous; so that the righteous won't use their hands to do evil. Do good, LORD, to those who are good, to those who are upright in their hearts.

But as for those who turn aside to their crooked ways, the LORD will lead them away with evildoers. Peace be on Israel.

PSALM 125

CHAPTER 57

LORD, my heart isn't haughty, nor my eyes lofty; nor do I concern myself with great matters, or things too wonderful for me.

Surely I have stilled and quieted my soul, like a weaned child with his mother, like a weaned child is my soul within me.

Israel, hope in the LORD, from this time forth and forevermore.

PSALM 131

PRAISE & WORSHIP HYMNS

CHAPTER 58

LORD, our Lord, how majestic is your name in all the earth. You have put your glory upon the heavens. From the lips of children and infants you have established praise, because of your adversaries, that you might silence the enemy and the avenger.

When I consider your heavens, the work of your fingers, the moon and the stars, which you have ordained; what is man, that you think of him, and the son of man that you care for him?

For you have made him a little lower than the angels. You have crowned him with glory and honor, and you made him ruler over the works of your hands. You have put all things under his feet: all sheep and cattle, and also the wild animals, the birds of the sky, and the fish of the sea, whatever passes through the paths of the seas.

LORD, our Lord, how majestic is your name in all the earth.

PSALM 8

CHAPTER 59

Ascribe to the LORD, you sons of the mighty, ascribe to the LORD glory and strength. Ascribe to the LORD the glory due to his name. Worship the LORD in holy array. The voice of the LORD is on the waters. The God of glory thunders, even the LORD on many waters.

The voice of the LORD is powerful. The voice of the LORD is full of majesty. The voice of the LORD breaks the cedars. Yes, the LORD breaks in pieces the cedars of Lebanon. He makes them also to skip like a calf; Lebanon and Sirion like a young, wild ox. The voice of the LORD strikes with flashes of lightning.

The voice of the LORD shakes the wilderness. The LORD shakes the wilderness of Kadesh. The voice of the LORD makes the deer give birth, and strips the forests bare. In his temple everything says, "Glory." The LORD sat enthroned at the Flood. Yes, the LORD sits as King forever.

The LORD will give strength to his people. The LORD will bless his people with peace.

PSALM 29

CHAPTER 60

Rejoice in the LORD, you righteous. Praise is fitting for the upright. Give thanks to the LORD with the lyre. Sing praises to him with the harp of ten strings. Sing to him a new song. Play skillfully with a shout of joy. For the word of the LORD is right. All his work is done in faithfulness. He loves righteousness and justice.

The earth is full of the loving kindness of the LORD. By the LORD's word, the heavens were made; all their army by the breath of his mouth. He gathers the waters of the sea together as a heap. He lays up the deeps in storehouses. Let all the earth fear the LORD. Let all the inhabitants of the world stand in awe of him.

For he spoke, and it was done. He commanded, and it stood firm. The LORD nullifies the counsel of the nations. He makes the thoughts of the peoples to be of no effect. The counsel of the LORD stands fast forever, the thoughts of his heart to all generations. Blessed is the nation whose God is the LORD, the people whom he has chosen for his own inheritance.

The LORD looks from heaven. He sees all the sons of men. From the place of his habitation he looks out on all the inhabitants of the earth, he who fashions all of their hearts; and he considers all of their works. There is no king saved by the multitude of an army.

A mighty man is not delivered by great strength. A horse is a vain thing for safety, neither does he deliver any by his great power. Look, the LORD's eye is on those who fear him, on those who hope in his loving kindness; to deliver their soul from death, to keep them alive in famine. Our soul waits for the LORD.

He is our help and our shield. For our heart rejoices in him, because we have trusted in his holy name. Let your loving kindness be on us, LORD, since we have hoped in you.

PSALM 33

CHAPTER 61

We have heard with our ears, God; our fathers have told us, what work you did in their days, in the days of old. You drove out the nations with your hand, but you planted them. You afflicted the peoples, but you spread them abroad.

For they did not get the land in possession by their own sword, neither did their own arm save them; but your right hand, and your arm, and the light of your face, because you were favorable to them. You are my King, my God, who commands victories for Jacob. Through you we will push back our adversaries. Through your name we will trample down those who rise up against us.

For I will not trust in my bow, neither shall my sword save me. But you have saved us from our adversaries, and have shamed those who hate us. In God we have made our boast all day long, we will give thanks to your name forever. Selah. But now you rejected us, and brought us to dishonor, and do not go out with our armies.

You make us turn back from the adversary. Those who hate us take spoil for themselves. You have made us like sheep for food, and have scattered us among the nations. You sell your people for nothing, and have gained nothing from their sale. You make us a reproach to our neighbors, a scoffing and a derision to those who are around us. You make us a byword among the nations, a shaking of the head among the peoples.

All day long my dishonor is before me, and shame covers my face, at the taunt of one who reproaches and verbally abuses, because of the enemy and the avenger. All this has come on us, yet have we not forgotten you, neither have we been false to your covenant.

Our heart has not turned back, neither have our steps strayed from your path, though you have crushed us in the haunt of jackals, and covered us with the shadow of death. If we have forgotten the name of our God, or spread forth our hands to a strange god; won't God search this out?

For he knows the secrets of the heart. For your sake we are killed all day long. We are regarded as sheep for the slaughter. Wake up. Why do you sleep, Lord? Arise. Do not reject us forever. Why do you hide your face, and forget our affliction and our oppression?

For our soul is bowed down to the dust. Our body cleaves to the earth. Rise up to help us. Redeem us for your loving kindness' sake.

PSALM 44

CHAPTER 62

God is our refuge and strength, a very present help in trouble. Therefore we won't be afraid, though the earth changes, though the mountains are shaken into the heart of the seas; though its waters roar and are troubled, though the mountains tremble with their swelling. Selah.

There is a river, the streams of which make the city of God glad, the holy place of the tents of the Most High. God is in her midst. She shall not be moved. God will help her at dawn. The nations raged. The kingdoms were moved. He lifted his voice, and the earth melted.

The LORD of hosts is with us. The God of Jacob is our refuge. Selah. Come, see the LORD's works, what desolations he has made in the earth. He makes wars cease to the end of the earth. He breaks the bow, and shatters the spear. He burns the chariots in the fire.

"Be still, and know that I am God. I will be exalted among the nations. I will be exalted in the earth." The LORD of hosts is with us. The God of Jacob is our refuge. Selah.

PSALM 46

CHAPTER 63

Oh clap your hands, all you nations. Shout to God with the voice of triumph. For the LORD Most High is awesome. He is a great King over all the earth. He subdues nations under us, and peoples under our feet. He chooses our inheritance for us, the glory of Jacob whom he loved. Selah.

God has gone up with a shout, the LORD with the sound of a trumpet. Sing praise to God, sing praises. Sing praises to our King, sing praises. For God is the King of all the earth. Sing praises with understanding. God reigns over the nations. God sits on his holy throne.

The princes of the peoples are gathered together, the people of the God of Abraham. For the shields of the earth belong to God. He is greatly exalted.

PSALM 47

CHAPTER 64

Great is the LORD, and greatly to be praised, in the city of our God, in his holy mountain. Beautiful in elevation, the joy of the whole earth, is Mount Zion, in the far north, the city of the great King.

God has shown himself in her citadels as a refuge. For, look, the kings assembled themselves, they passed by together. They saw it, then they were amazed. They were dismayed. They hurried away. Trembling took hold of them there, pain, as of a woman in travail.

With the east wind, you break the ships of Tarshish. As we have heard, so we have seen, in the city of the LORD of hosts, in the city of our God. God will establish it forever. Selah. We have thought about your loving kindness, God, in the midst of your temple.

As is your name, God, so is your praise to the farthest parts of the earth. Your right hand is full of righteousness. Let Mount Zion be glad. Let the daughters of Judah rejoice, Because of your judgments. Walk about Zion, and go around her. Number its towers.

Consider her defenses. Consider her palaces, that you may tell it to the next generation. For this God is our God forever and ever. He will be our guide even to death.

PSALM 48

CHAPTER 65

Have mercy on me, God, according to your loving kindness. According to the multitude of your tender mercies, blot out my transgressions. Wash me thoroughly from my iniquity. Cleanse me from my sin. For I know my transgressions.

My sin is constantly before me. Against you, and you only, have I sinned, and done that which is evil in your sight; that you may be proved right when you speak, and justified when you judge. Look, I was brought forth in iniquity. In sin my mother conceived me. Look, you desire truth in the inward parts. You teach me wisdom in the inmost place. Purify me with hyssop, and I will be clean. Wash me, and I will be whiter than snow.

Let me hear joy and gladness, that the bones which you have broken may rejoice. Hide your face from my sins, and blot out all of my iniquities. Create in me a clean heart, O God. Renew a right spirit within me. Do not throw me from your presence, and do not take your Holy Spirit from me.

Restore to me the joy of your salvation. Uphold me with a willing spirit. Then I will teach transgressors your ways. Sinners shall be converted to you. Deliver me from bloodguiltiness, O God, the God of my salvation.

My tongue shall sing aloud of your righteousness. Lord, open my lips. My mouth shall declare your praise.

For you do not delight in sacrifice, or else I would give it. You have no pleasure in burnt offering. The sacrifices of God are a broken spirit. A broken and contrite heart, O God, you will not despise.

Do well in your good pleasure to Zion. Build the walls of Jerusalem. Then you will delight in the sacrifices of righteousness, in burnt offerings and in whole burnt offerings. Then they will offer bulls on your altar.

PSALM 51

CHAPTER 66

Do you indeed speak righteousness, silent ones? Do you judge blamelessly, you sons of men? No, in your heart you plot injustice. You measure out the violence of your hands in the earth. The wicked go astray from the womb. They are wayward as soon as they are born, speaking lies.

Their poison is like the poison of a serpent; like a deaf viper that stops its ear, which doesn't listen to the voice of charmers, no matter how skillful the charmer may be. Break their teeth, God, in their mouth. Break out the great teeth of the young lions, LORD. Let them vanish as water that flows away.

When they draw the bow, let their arrows be made blunt. Let them be like a snail which melts and passes away, like the stillborn child, who has not seen the sun. Before your pots can feel the heat of the thorns, he will sweep away the green and the burning alike.

The righteous shall rejoice when he sees the vengeance. He shall wash his feet in the blood of the wicked; so that men shall say, "Most certainly there is a reward for the righteous. Most certainly there is a God who judges the earth."

PSALM 58

CHAPTER 67

God, you have rejected us. You have broken us down. You have been angry. Restore us, again. You have made the land tremble. You have torn it. Mend its fractures, for it quakes. You have shown your people hard things. You have made us drink the wine that makes us stagger.

You have given a banner to those who fear you, that it may be displayed because of the truth. Selah. So that your beloved may be delivered, save with your right hand and answer me. God has spoken from his sanctuary: "I will triumph. I will divide Shechem, and measure out the valley of Succoth. Gilead is mine, and Manasseh is mine.

Ephraim also is the defense of my head. Judah is my scepter. Moab is my wash basin. I will throw my shoe on Edom. I shout in triumph over Philistia." Who will bring me into the strong city? Who will lead me to Edom? Haven't you, God, rejected us? You do not go out with our armies, God.

Give us help against the adversary, for the help of man is vain. Through God we shall do valiantly, for it is he who will tread down our adversaries.

PSALM 60

CHAPTER 68

Let God arise. Let his enemies be scattered, and let them who hate him flee before him. As smoke is driven away, so drive them away. As wax melts before the fire, so let the wicked perish at the presence of God. But let the righteous be glad. Let them rejoice before God. Yes, let them rejoice with gladness.

Sing to God. Sing praises to his name. Extol him who rides on the clouds: to the LORD, his name. Rejoice before him. A father of the fatherless, and a defender of the widows, is God in his holy habitation. God sets the lonely in families. He brings out the prisoners with singing, but the rebellious dwell in a sun-scorched land.

God, when you went forth before your people, when you marched through the wilderness... Selah. The earth trembled. The sky also poured down rain at the presence of the God of Sinai — at the presence of God, the God of Israel. You, God, sent a plentiful rain. You confirmed your inheritance, when it was weary. Your congregation lived in it. You, God, prepared your goodness for the poor.

The Lord announced the word. The ones who proclaim it are a great company. "Kings of armies flee. They flee." She who waits at home divides the spoil, while you sleep among the campfires, the wings of a dove sheathed with silver, her feathers with shining gold. When Shaddai scattered kings in her, it snowed on Zalmon.

The mountains of Bashan are majestic mountains. The mountains of Bashan are rugged. Why do you look in envy, you rugged mountains, at the mountain where God chooses to reign? Yes, the LORD will dwell there forever. The chariots of God are tens of thousands and thousands of thousands. The Lord is among them, from Sinai, in holiness.

You have ascended on high. You have led away captives. And you gave gifts to people; but the rebellious will not dwell in the presence of God. Blessed be the Lord, who daily bears our burdens, even the God who is our salvation. Selah. God is to us a God of deliverance. To the LORD, the Lord, belongs escape from death. But God will strike through the head of his enemies, the hairy scalp of such a one as still continues in his guiltiness.

The Lord said, "I will bring you again from Bashan, I will bring you again from the depths of the sea; that you may crush them, dipping your foot in blood, that the tongues of your dogs may have their portion from your enemies." They have seen your processions, God, even the processions of my God, my King, into the sanctuary.

The singers went before, the minstrels followed after, in the midst of the ladies playing with tambourines, "Bless God in the congregations, even the Lord in the assembly of Israel." There is little Benjamin, their ruler, the princes of Judah, their council, the princes of Zebulun, and the princes of Naphtali. Your God has commanded your strength. Strengthen, God, that which you have done for us.

Because of your temple at Jerusalem, kings shall bring presents to you. Rebuke the wild animal of the reeds, the multitude of the bulls, with the calves of the peoples. Being humbled, may it bring bars of silver. Scatter the nations that delight in war. Envoys shall come out of Egypt. Ethiopia shall hurry to stretch out her hands to God.

Sing to God, you kingdoms of the earth. Sing praises to the Lord. Selah. To him who rides on the heaven of heavens, which are of old; look, he utters his voice, a mighty voice. Ascribe strength to God. His excellency is over Israel, his strength is in the skies. You are awesome, God, in your sanctuaries. The God of Israel gives strength and power to his people. Praise be to God.

PSALM 68

CHAPTER 69

In Judah, God is known. His name is great in Israel. And his abode is in Salem, and his lair in Zion. There he broke the flaming arrows of the bow, the shield, and the sword, and the weapons of war. Selah. Glorious are you, and excellent, more than mountains of game. Valiant men lie plundered, they have slept their last sleep.

None of the men of war can lift their hands. At your rebuke, God of Jacob, both chariot and horse are cast into a deep sleep. You, even you, are to be feared. Who can stand in your sight when you are angry? You pronounced judgment from heaven. The earth feared, and was silent, when God arose to judgment, to save all the afflicted ones of the earth. Selah. Surely the wrath of man praises you.

The survivors of your wrath are restrained. Make vows to the LORD your God, and fulfill them. Let all of his neighbors bring presents to him who is to be feared. He humbles the spirit of princes. He is feared by the kings of the earth.

PSALM 76

CHAPTER 70

God, the nations have come into your inheritance. They have defiled your holy temple. They have laid Jerusalem in heaps. They have given the dead bodies of your servants to be food for the birds of the sky, the flesh of your faithful to the animals of the earth. Their blood they have shed like water around Jerusalem.

There was no one to bury them. We have become a reproach to our neighbors, a scoffing and derision to those who are around us. How long, LORD? Will you be angry forever? Will your jealousy burn like fire? Pour out your wrath on the nations that do not know you; on the kingdoms that do not call on your name; for they have devoured Jacob, and destroyed his homeland.

Do not hold the iniquities of our forefathers against us. Let your tender mercies speedily meet us, for we are in desperate need. Help us, God of our salvation, for the glory of your name. Deliver us, and forgive our sins, for your name's sake. Why should the nations say, "Where is their God?" Let it be known among the nations, before our eyes, that vengeance for your servants' blood is being poured out. Let the sighing of the prisoner come before you.

According to the greatness of your power, free those who are sentenced to death. Pay back to our neighbors seven times into their bosom their reproach with which they have reproached you, Lord. So we, your people and sheep of your pasture, will give you thanks forever. We will praise you forever, to all generations.

PSALM 79

CHAPTER 71

Hear us, Shepherd of Israel, you who lead Joseph like a flock, you who sit above the cherubim, shine forth. Before Ephraim and Benjamin and Manasseh, stir up your might. Come to save us. Restore us, God. Cause your face to shine, and we will be saved. LORD God of hosts, How long will you be angry against the prayer of your people? You have fed them with the bread of tears, and given them tears to drink in large measure.

You make us a source of contention to our neighbors. Our enemies have mocked us. Restore us, God of hosts. Cause your face to shine, and we will be saved. You brought a vine out of Egypt. You drove out the nations, and planted it. You cleared the ground for it. It took deep root, and filled the land. The mountains were covered with its shadow. Its boughs were like God's cedars. It sent out its branches to the sea, its shoots to the River.

Why have you broken down its walls, so that all those who pass by the way pluck it? The boar out of the wood ravages it. The wild animals of the field feed on it. Return, we beg you, God of hosts. Look down from heaven, and see, and visit this vine, the stock which your right hand planted, the branch that you made strong for yourself. It's burned with fire. It's cut down. They perish at your rebuke.

Let your hand be on the man of your right hand, on the son of man whom you made strong for yourself. So we will not turn away from you. Revive us, and we will call on your name. Restore us, LORD God of hosts. Cause your face to shine, and we will be saved.

PSALM 80

CHAPTER 72

God presides in the assembly of God. He judges among the gods. "How long will you judge unjustly, and show partiality to the wicked?" Selah. "Defend the weak, the poor, and the fatherless. Maintain the rights of the poor and oppressed. Rescue the weak and needy. Deliver them out of the hand of the wicked."

They do not know, neither do they understand. They walk back and forth in darkness. All the foundations of the earth are shaken. I said, "You are gods, all of you are sons of the Most High. Nevertheless you shall die like men, and fall like one of the rulers." Arise, God, judge the earth, for you inherit all of the nations.

PSALM 82

CHAPTER 73

How lovely are your dwellings, LORD of hosts. My soul longs, yes, yearns for the courts of the LORD. My heart and my flesh cry out for the living God. Yes, the sparrow has found a home, and the swallow a nest for herself, where she may have her young, near your altars, LORD of hosts, my King, and my God.

Blessed are those who dwell in your house. They are ever praising you. Selah. Blessed are those whose strength is in you, who have set their hearts on a pilgrimage. Passing through the valley of Weeping, they make it a place of springs. Yes, the autumn rain covers it with blessings. They go from strength to strength. Everyone of them appears before God in Zion.

LORD, God of hosts, hear my prayer. Listen, God of Jacob. Selah. Look, God our shield, look at the face of your anointed. For a day in your courts is better than a thousand. I would rather be a doorkeeper in the house of God, than to dwell in the tents of wickedness.

For the LORD God is a sun and a shield. The LORD will give grace and glory. He withholds no good thing from those who walk blamelessly. LORD of hosts, blessed is the man who trusts in you.

PSALM 84

CHAPTER 74

LORD, you have been favorable to your land. You have restored the fortunes of Jacob. You have forgiven the iniquity of your people. You have covered all their sin. Selah. You have taken away all your wrath. You have turned from the fierceness of your anger.

Turn us, God of our salvation, and cause your indignation toward us to cease. Will you be angry with us forever? Will you draw out your anger to all generations? Won't you revive us again, that your people may rejoice in you? Show us your loving kindness, LORD.

Grant us your salvation. I will hear what God, the LORD, will speak, for he will speak peace to his people, his faithful ones; but let them not turn again to folly. Surely his salvation is near those who fear him, that glory may dwell in our land. Mercy and truth meet together. Righteousness and peace have kissed each other.

Truth springs out of the earth. Righteousness has looked down from heaven. Yes, the LORD will give that which is good. Our land will yield its increase. Righteousness goes before him, and prepares the way for his steps.

PSALM 85

CHAPTER 75

His foundation is in the holy mountains. The LORD loves the gates of Zion more than all the dwellings of Jacob. Glorious things are spoken about you, city of God. Selah. I will record Rahab and Babylon among those who acknowledge me. Look, Philistia, Tyre, and also Ethiopia: "This one was born there."

Yes, of Zion it will be said, "This one and that one was born in her;" the Most High himself will establish her. The LORD will count, when he writes up the peoples, "This one was born there." Selah. Those who sing as well as those who dance say, "All my springs are in you."

PSALM 87

CHAPTER 76

Lord, you have been our dwelling place for all generations. Before the mountains were brought forth, before you had formed the earth and the world, even from everlasting to everlasting, you are God. You turn man to destruction, saying, "Return, you children of men." For a thousand years in your sight are just like yesterday when it is past, like a watch in the night.

You sweep them away as they sleep. In the morning they sprout like new grass. In the morning it sprouts and springs up. By evening, it is withered and dry. For we are consumed in your anger. We are troubled in your wrath. You have set our iniquities before you, our secret sins in the light of your presence. For all our days have passed away in your wrath. We bring our years to an end as a sigh.

The days of our years are seventy, or even by reason of strength eighty years; yet their pride is but labor and sorrow, for it passes quickly, and we fly away. Who knows the power of your anger, your wrath according to the fear that is due to you? So teach us to number our days, that we may gain a heart of wisdom. Relent, LORD. How long?

Have compassion on your servants. Satisfy us in the morning with your loving kindness, that we may rejoice and be glad all our days. Make us glad for as many days as you have afflicted us, for as many years as we have seen evil. Let your work appear to your servants; your glory to their children.

Let the favor of the Lord our God be on us; establish the work of our hands for us; yes, establish the work of our hands.

PSALM 90

CHAPTER 77

LORD, you God to whom vengeance belongs, you God to whom vengeance belongs, shine forth. Rise up, you judge of the earth. Pay back the proud what they deserve. LORD, how long will the wicked, how long will the wicked triumph? They pour out arrogant words. All the evildoers boast. They break your people in pieces, LORD, and afflict your heritage.

They kill the widow and the alien, and murder the fatherless. They say, "The LORD will not see, neither will Jacob's God consider." Consider, you senseless among the people; you fools, when will you be wise? He who implanted the ear, won't he hear? He who formed the eye, won't he see? He who disciplines the nations, won't he punish? He who teaches man knows. The LORD knows the thoughts of man, that they are futile.

Blessed is the man whom you discipline, LORD, and teach out of your Law; that you may give him rest from the days of adversity, until the pit is dug for the wicked. For the LORD won't reject his people, neither will he forsake his inheritance. For judgment will return to righteousness. All the upright in heart shall follow it. Who will rise up for me against the wicked? Who will stand up for me against the evildoers?

Unless the LORD had been my help, my soul would have soon lived in silence. When I said, "My foot is slipping." Your loving kindness, LORD, held me up. In the multitude of my thoughts within me, your comforts delight my soul. Shall the throne of wickedness have fellowship with you, which brings about mischief by statute?

They gather themselves together against the soul of the righteous, and condemn the innocent blood. But the LORD has been my high tower, my God, the rock of my refuge. He has brought on them their own iniquity, and will cut them off in their own wickedness. The LORD, our God, will cut them off.

PSALM 94

CHAPTER 78

Oh come, let's sing to the LORD. Let's shout aloud to the rock of our salvation. Let's come before his presence with thanksgiving. Let's extol him with songs. For the LORD is a great God, a great King above all gods. In his hand are the deep places of the earth. The heights of the mountains are also his. The sea is his, and he made it. His hands formed the dry land.

Oh come, let's worship and bow down. Let's kneel before the LORD, our Maker, for he is our God. We are the people of his pasture, and the sheep in his care. Today, if you would hear his voice. Do not harden your heart, as at Meribah, as in the day of Massah in the wilderness, when your fathers tempted me, tested me, and saw my work. Forty long years I was grieved with that generation, and said, "It is a people that errs in their heart. They have not known my ways." Therefore I swore in my wrath, "They won't enter into my rest."

PSALM 95

CHAPTER 79

Sing to the LORD a new song, for he has done marvelous things. His right hand, and his holy arm, have worked salvation for him. The LORD has made known his salvation. He has openly shown his righteousness in the sight of the nations. He has remembered his loving kindness and his faithfulness toward the house of Israel. Every part of the earth has seen the salvation of our God.

Make a joyful noise to the LORD, all the earth. Burst out and sing for joy, yes, sing praises. Sing praises to the LORD with the harp, with the harp and the voice of melody. With trumpets and sound of the ram's horn, make a joyful noise before the King, the LORD. Let the sea roar with its fullness; the world, and those who dwell in it. Let the rivers clap their hands. Let the mountains sing for joy together. Let them sing before the LORD, for he comes to judge the earth. He will judge the world with righteousness, and the peoples with equity.

PSALM 98

CHAPTER 80

Shout for joy to the LORD, all you lands. Serve the LORD with gladness. Come before his presence with singing. Know that the LORD, he is God. It is he who has made us, and not we ourselves.

We are his people, and the sheep of his pasture. Enter into his gates with thanksgiving, and into his courts with praise. Give thanks to him, and bless his name. For the LORD is good. His loving kindness endures forever, and his faithfulness to all generations.

PSALM 100

CHAPTER 81

Hear my prayer, LORD. Let my cry come to you. Do not hide your face from me in the day of my distress. Turn your ear to me. Answer me quickly in the day when I call. For my days consume away like smoke. My bones are burned like a hearth. My heart is blighted like grass, and withered, for I forget to eat my bread. By reason of the voice of my groaning, my bones stick to my skin.

I am like a pelican of the wilderness. I have become as an owl of the waste places. I watch, and have become like a sparrow that is alone on the housetop. My enemies reproach me all day. Those who are mad at me use my name as a curse. For I have eaten ashes like bread, and mixed my drink with tears, Because of your indignation and your wrath, for you have taken me up, and thrown me away. My days are like a long shadow. I have withered like grass.

But you, LORD, will abide forever; your renown endures to all generations. You will arise and have mercy on Zion; for it is time to have pity on her. Yes, the set time has come. For your servants take pleasure in her stones, and have pity on her dust. So the nations will fear the name of the LORD; all the kings of the earth your glory. For the LORD has built up Zion. He has appeared in his glory.

He has responded to the prayer of the destitute, and has not despised their prayer. This will be written for the generation to come, that a people yet to be created may praise the LORD. For he has looked down from the height of his sanctuary.

From heaven, the LORD looked at the earth; to hear the groans of the prisoner; to free those who are condemned to death; that men may declare the name of the LORD in Zion, and his praise in Jerusalem; when the peoples are gathered together, the kingdoms, to serve the LORD.

He weakened my strength along the course. He shortened my days. I said, "My God, do not take me away in the midst of my days. Your years are throughout all generations. In the beginning, LORD, you established the foundation of the earth. The heavens are the works of your hands. They will perish, but you remain; and they will all wear out like a garment.

You will change them like a cloak, and they will be changed. But you are the same. Your years will have no end. The children of your servants will continue, and their descendants will be established before you."

PSALM 102

CHAPTER 82

Praise the LORD, my soul, and all that is within me, praise his holy name. Praise the LORD, my soul, and do not forget all his benefits; who forgives all your sins; who heals all your diseases; who redeems your life from destruction; who crowns you with loving kindness and tender mercies; who satisfies your desire with good things; your youth is renewed like the eagle's.

The LORD executes righteous acts, and justice for all who are oppressed. He made known his ways to Moses, his deeds to the children of Israel. The LORD is merciful and gracious, slow to anger, and abundant in loving kindness. He will not always accuse; neither will he stay angry forever. He has not dealt with us according to our sins, nor repaid us for our iniquities.

For as the heavens are high above the earth, so great is his loving kindness toward those who fear him. As far as the east is from the west, so far has he removed our transgressions from us. Like a father has compassion on his children, so the LORD has compassion on those who fear him. For he knows how we are made. He remembers that we are dust.

As for man, his days are like grass. As a flower of the field, so he flourishes. For the wind passes over it, and it is gone, and its place remembers it no more.

But the LORD's loving kindness is from everlasting to everlasting with those who fear him, his righteousness to children's children; to those who keep his covenant, to those who remember to obey his precepts.

The LORD has established his throne in the heavens. His kingdom rules over all. Praise the LORD, all you angels of his, who are mighty in strength, who fulfill his word, obeying the voice of his word. Praise the LORD, all you armies of his, you servants of his, who do his pleasure. Praise the LORD, all you works of his, in all places of his dominion. Praise the LORD, my soul.

PSALM 103

CHAPTER 83

Bless the LORD, my soul. The LORD, my God, you are very great. You are clothed with splendor and majesty. He covers himself with light as with a garment. He stretches out the heavens like a curtain. He lays the beams of his chambers in the waters. He makes the clouds his chariot. He walks on the wings of the wind.

He makes his angels winds, and his servants flames of fire. He laid the foundations of the earth, that it should not be moved forever and ever. You covered it with the deep as with a cloak. The waters stood above the mountains. At your rebuke they fled. At the voice of your thunder they hurried away. The mountains rose, the valleys sank down, to the place which you had assigned to them.

You have set a boundary that they may not pass over; that they do not turn again to cover the earth. He sends forth springs into the valleys. They run among the mountains. They give drink to every animal of the field. The wild donkeys quench their thirst. The birds of the sky nest by them; among the branches they give forth a sound.

He waters the mountains from his chambers. The earth is filled with the fruit of your works. He causes the grass to grow for the livestock, and plants for man to cultivate, that he may bring forth food out of the earth: wine that makes glad the heart of man, oil to make his face to shine, and bread that strengthens man's heart.

The LORD's trees are well watered, the cedars of Lebanon, which he has planted; where the birds make their nests. The stork makes its home in the fir trees. The high mountains are for the wild goats. The rocks are a refuge for the rock badgers. He appointed the moon for seasons. The sun knows when to set.

You make darkness, and it is night, in which all the animals of the forest prowl. The young lions roar after their prey, and seek their food from God. The sun rises, and they steal away, and lie down in their dens. Man goes forth to his work, to his labor until the evening. LORD, how many are your works. In wisdom have you made them all. The earth is full of your riches.

There is the sea, great and wide, in which are innumerable living things, both small and large animals. There the ships go, and leviathan, whom you formed to play there. These all wait for you, that you may give them their food in due season. You give to them; they gather. You open your hand; they are satisfied with good.

You hide your face: they are troubled; you take away their breath: they die, and return to the dust. You send forth your Spirit: they are created. You renew the face of the ground. Let the glory of the LORD endure forever. Let the LORD rejoice in his works. He looks at the earth, and it trembles. He touches the mountains, and they smoke.

I will sing to the LORD all my life. I will sing praise to my God as long as I exist. Let your meditation be sweet to him. I will rejoice in the LORD. Let sinners be consumed out of the earth. Let the wicked be no more. Bless the LORD, my soul. Praise the LORD.

PSALM 104

CHAPTER 84

My heart is steadfast, God. I will sing and I will make music with my soul. Wake up, harp and lyre. I will wake up the dawn. I will give thanks to you, LORD, among the nations. I will sing praises to you among the peoples. For your loving kindness is great above the heavens. Your faithfulness reaches to the skies.

Be exalted, God, above the heavens. Let your glory be over all the earth. That your beloved may be delivered, save with your right hand, and answer us. God has spoken from his sanctuary: "In triumph, I will divide Shechem, and measure out the valley of Succoth. Gilead is mine. Manasseh is mine. Ephraim also is my helmet. Judah is my scepter. Moab is my wash pot.

I will toss my sandal on Edom. I will shout in triumph over Philistia." Who will bring me into the fortified city? Who has led me to Edom? Haven't you rejected us, God? You do not go forth, God, with our armies. Give us help against the enemy, for the help of man is vain. Through God, we will do valiantly. For it is he who will trample down our enemies.

PSALM 108

CHAPTER 85

Praise the LORD. I will give thanks to the LORD with my whole heart, in the council of the upright, and in the congregation. The LORD's works are great, pondered by all those who delight in them. His work is honor and majesty. His righteousness endures forever. He has caused his wonderful works to be remembered.

The LORD is gracious and merciful. He has given food to those who fear him. He always remembers his covenant. He has shown his people the power of his works, in giving them the heritage of the nations. The works of his hands are truth and justice. All his precepts are sure. They are established forever and ever. They are done in truth and uprightness. He has sent redemption to his people.

He has ordained his covenant forever. His name is holy and awesome. The fear of the LORD is the beginning of wisdom. All those who do his work have a good understanding. His praise endures forever.

PSALM 111

CHAPTER 86

Praise the LORD. Praise, you servants of the LORD, praise the name of the LORD. Blessed be the name of the LORD, from this time forth and forevermore. From the rising of the sun to the going down of the same, The LORD's name is to be praised.

The LORD is high above all nations, his glory above the heavens. Who is like the LORD, our God, who has his seat on high, who stoops down to see in heaven and in the earth? He raises up the poor out of the dust. Lifts up the needy from the ash heap; that he may set him with princes, even with the princes of his people.

He settles the barren woman in her home, as a joyful mother of children. Praise the LORD.

PSALM 113

CHAPTER 87

When Israel went forth out of Egypt, the house of Jacob from a people of foreign language; Judah became his sanctuary, Israel his dominion. The sea saw it, and fled. The Jordan was driven back. The mountains skipped like rams, the little hills like lambs.

What was it, you sea, that you fled? You Jordan, that you turned back? You mountains, that you skipped like rams; you little hills, like lambs? Tremble, you earth, at the presence of the Lord, at the presence of the God of Jacob, who turned the rock into a pool of water, the flint into a spring of waters.

PSALM 114

CHAPTER 88

Not to us, LORD, not to us, but to your name give glory, for your loving kindness, and for your truth's sake. Why should the nations say, "Where is their God, now?" But our God is in the heavens. He does whatever he pleases.

Their idols are silver and gold, the work of men's hands. They have mouths, but they do not speak. They have eyes, but they do not see. They have ears, but they do not hear. They have noses, but they do not smell. They have hands, but they do not feel. They have feet, but they do not walk, neither do they speak through their throat. Those who make them will be like them; yes, everyone who trusts in them. Israel, trust in the LORD.

He is their help and their shield. House of Aaron, trust in the LORD. He is their help and their shield. You who fear the LORD, trust in the LORD. He is their help and their shield. The LORD remembers us. He will bless us. He will bless the house of Israel. He will bless the house of Aaron. He will bless those who fear the LORD, both small and great. May the LORD increase you more and more, you and your children.

Blessed are you by the LORD, who made heaven and earth. The heavens are the heavens of the LORD; but the earth has he given to the children of men.

The dead do not praise the LORD, neither any who go down into silence; but we will bless the LORD, from this time forth and forevermore. Praise the LORD.

PSALM 115

CHAPTER 89

Praise the LORD, all you nations. Praise him, all you peoples. For his loving kindness is great toward us. The LORD's faithfulness endures forever. Praise the LORD.

PSALM 117

CHAPTER 90

I was glad when they said to me, "Let's go to the LORD's house." Our feet are standing within your gates, Jerusalem; Jerusalem, that is built as a city that is compact together; where the tribes go up, even the tribes of the LORD, according to an ordinance for Israel, to give thanks to the name of the LORD. For there are set thrones for judgment, the thrones of David's house.

Pray for the peace of Jerusalem. Those who love you will prosper. Peace be within your walls, and prosperity within your palaces. For my brothers' and companions' sakes, I will now say, "Peace be within you." For the sake of the house of the LORD our God, I will seek your good.

PSALM 122

CHAPTER 91

To you I do lift up my eyes, you who sit in the heavens. Look, as the eyes of servants look to the hand of their master, as the eyes of a maid to the hand of her mistress; so our eyes look to the LORD, our God, until he has mercy on us.

Have mercy on us, LORD, have mercy on us, for we have endured much contempt. Our soul is exceedingly filled with the scoffing of those who are at ease, with the contempt of the proud.

PSALM 123

CHAPTER 92

When the LORD brought back those who returned to Zion, we were like those who dream. Then our mouth was filled with laughter, and our tongue with singing. Then they said among the nations, "The LORD has done great things for them."

The LORD has done great things for us, and we are glad. Restore our fortunes again, LORD, like the streams in the Negev. Those who sow in tears will reap in joy. He who goes out weeping, carrying seed for sowing, will certainly come again with joy, carrying his sheaves.

PSALM 126

CHAPTER 93

Look. Praise the LORD, all you servants of the LORD, who stand by night in the LORD's house. Lift up your hands in the sanctuary. Praise the LORD. May the LORD bless you from Zion; even he who made heaven and earth.

PSALM 134

CHAPTER 94

Praise the LORD. Praise the name of the LORD. Praise him, you servants of the LORD, you who stand in the house of the LORD, in the courts of our God's house. Praise the LORD, for the LORD is good. Sing praises to his name, for that is pleasant. For the LORD has chosen Jacob for himself; Israel for his own possession. For I know that the LORD is great, that our Lord is above all gods.

Whatever the LORD pleased, that he has done, in heaven and in earth, in the seas and in all deeps; who causes the clouds to rise from the farthest parts of the earth; who makes lightnings with the rain; who brings forth the wind out of his treasuries; Who struck the firstborn of Egypt, both of man and animal;

Who sent signs and wonders into the midst of you, Egypt, on Pharaoh, and on all his servants; who struck many nations, and killed mighty kings, Sihon king of the Amorites, Og king of Bashan, and all the kingdoms of Canaan, and gave their land for a heritage, a heritage to Israel, his people.

Your name, LORD, endures forever; your renown, LORD, throughout all generations. For the LORD will judge his people, and have compassion on his servants. The idols of the nations are silver and gold, the work of men's hands. They have mouths, but they can't speak. They have eyes, but they can't see.

They have ears, but they can't hear; neither is there any breath in their mouths. Those who make them will be like them; yes, everyone who trusts in them. House of Israel, praise the LORD. House of Aaron, praise the LORD. House of Levi, praise the LORD. You who fear the LORD, praise the LORD. Blessed be the LORD from Zion, Who dwells at Jerusalem. Praise the LORD.

PSALM 135

CHAPTER 95

By the rivers of Babylon, there we sat down. Yes, we wept, when we remembered Zion. On the willows in its midst, we hung up our harps. For there, those who led us captive asked us for songs. Those who tormented us demanded songs of joy: "Sing us one of the songs of Zion." How can we sing the LORD's song in a foreign land?

If I forget you, Jerusalem, let my right hand forget its skill. Let my tongue stick to the roof of my mouth if I do not remember you; if I do not prefer Jerusalem above my chief joy. Remember, LORD, against the children of Edom, the day of Jerusalem; who said, "Raze it. Raze it even to its foundation."

Daughter of Babylon, doomed to destruction, he will be blessed who rewards you, as you have served us. Blessed shall he be who takes and dashes your little ones against the rock.

PSALM 137

CHAPTER 96

I will exalt you, my God, the King. I will praise your name forever and ever. Every day I will praise you. I will extol your name forever and ever. Great is the LORD, and greatly to be praised. His greatness is unsearchable. One generation will commend your works to another, and will declare your mighty acts. Of the glorious splendor of your majesty they will speak, of your wondrous works, I will meditate.

Men will speak of the might of your awesome acts. I will declare your greatness. They will utter the memory of your great goodness, and will sing of your righteousness. The LORD is gracious, merciful, slow to anger, and of great loving kindness. The LORD is good to all. His tender mercies are over all his works.

All your works will give thanks to you, LORD. And your faithful ones will bless you. They will speak of the glory of your kingdom, and talk about your power; to make known to the sons of men his mighty acts, the glory of the majesty of his kingdom. Your kingdom is an everlasting kingdom. Your dominion endures throughout all generations.

The LORD is faithful in all his words, and gracious in all his deeds. The LORD upholds all who fall, and raises up all those who are bowed down. The eyes of all wait for you. You give them their food in due season. You open your hand, and satisfy the desire of every living thing. The LORD is righteous in all his ways, and faithful in all his deeds.

The LORD is near to all those who call on him, to all who call on him in truth. He will fulfill the desire of those who fear him. He also will hear their cry, and will save them.

The LORD preserves all those who love him, but all the wicked he will destroy. My mouth will speak the praise of the LORD. Let all flesh bless his holy name forever and ever.

PSALM 145

CHAPTER 97

Praise the LORD. Praise the LORD, my soul. While I live, I will praise the LORD. I will sing praises to my God as long as I exist. Do not put your trust in princes, each a son of man in whom there is no help. His spirit departs, and he returns to the earth. In that very day, his thoughts perish.

Blessed is the one who has the God of Jacob for his help, whose hope is in the LORD his God, who made heaven and earth, the sea, and all that is in them; who keeps truth forever; who executes justice for the oppressed; who gives food to the hungry. The LORD frees the prisoners. The LORD opens the eyes of the blind. The LORD raises up those who are bowed down. The LORD loves the righteous.

The LORD preserves the foreigners. He upholds the fatherless and widow, but the way of the wicked he turns upside down. The LORD will reign forever; your God, O Zion, to all generations. Praise the LORD.

PSALM 146

CHAPTER 98

Praise the LORD, for it is good to sing praises to our God; for it is pleasant and fitting to praise him. The LORD builds up Jerusalem. He gathers together the outcasts of Israel. He heals the broken in heart, and binds up their wounds. He counts the number of the stars. He calls them all by their names. Great is our Lord, and mighty in power. His understanding is infinite.

The LORD upholds the humble. He brings the wicked down to the ground. Sing to the LORD with thanksgiving. Sing praises on the harp to our God, who covers the sky with clouds, who prepares rain for the earth, who makes grass grow on the mountains. He provides food for the livestock, and for the young ravens when they call.

He doesn't delight in the strength of the horse. He takes no pleasure in the legs of a man. The LORD takes pleasure in those who fear him, in those who hope in his loving kindness. Praise the LORD, Jerusalem. Praise your God, Zion. For he has strengthened the bars of your gates. He has blessed your children within you. He makes peace in your borders.

He fills you with the finest of the wheat. He sends out his commandment to the earth. His word runs very swiftly. He gives snow like wool, and scatters frost like ashes. He hurls down his hail like pebbles.

Who can stand before his cold? He sends out his word, and melts them. He causes his wind to blow, and the waters flow. He shows his word to Jacob; his statutes and his ordinances to Israel. He has not done this for just any nation. They do not know his ordinances. Praise the LORD.

PSALM 147

CHAPTER 99

Praise the LORD. Praise the LORD from the heavens. Praise him in the heights. Praise him, all his angels. Praise him, all his army. Praise him, sun and moon. Praise him, all you shining stars. Praise him, you heavens of heavens, You waters that are above the heavens. Let them praise the name of the LORD, for he commanded, and they were created. He has also established them forever and ever.

He has made a decree which will not pass away. Praise the LORD from the earth, you great sea creatures, and all depths. Lightning and hail, snow and clouds; stormy wind, fulfilling his word; mountains and all hills; fruit trees and all cedars; wild animals and all livestock; small creatures and flying birds; kings of the earth and all peoples; princes and all judges of the earth; both young men and maidens; old men and children: let them praise the name of the LORD, for his name alone is exalted.

His glory is above the earth and the heavens. He has lifted up the horn of his people, the praise of all his faithful ones; even of the children of Israel, a people near to him. Praise the LORD.

PSALM 148

CHAPTER 100

Praise the LORD. Sing to the LORD a new song, his praise in the assembly of the faithful ones. Let Israel rejoice in him who made them. Let the children of Zion be joyful in their King. Let them praise his name in the dance. Let them sing praises to him with tambourine and harp.

For the LORD takes pleasure in his people. He crowns the humble with salvation. Let the faithful ones rejoice in glory. Let them sing for joy on their beds. May the high praises of God be in their mouths, and a two-edged sword in their hand; to execute vengeance on the nations, and punishments on the peoples;

To bind their kings with chains, and their nobles with fetters of iron; to execute on them the written judgment. All his faithful ones have this honor. Praise the LORD.

PSALM 149

CHAPTER 101

Praise the LORD. Praise God in his sanctuary. Praise him in his heavens for his acts of power. Praise him for his mighty acts. Praise him according to his excellent greatness. Praise him with the sounding of the trumpet.

Praise him with harp and lyre. Praise him with tambourine and dancing. Praise him with stringed instruments and flute. Praise him with loud cymbals. Praise him with resounding cymbals. Let everything that has breath praise the LORD. Praise the LORD.

PSALM 150

WHAT DID YOU THINK ABOUT PSALMS WITH GOD'S WISDOM

Thank you for purchasing this book. I know you could have picked any number of books to read but you picked this book and for that I am extremely grateful.

I hope it added value and quality to your everyday life. If so, it would be really nice if you could share this book with your friends and family by posting to Facebook and Twitter.

If you enjoyed this book and found some benefit in reading it, I'd like to hear from you and hope that you could take some time to post a review.

I want you to know that your review is very important to me.

Thank you again & I wish you all the best as you journey wisely through life.

OTHER BOOKS TO CONSIDER

Proverbs with God's Wisdom: Navigating life wisely with 400+ quotes across 30+ topics from the Biblical book of Proverbs

If you are new to Audible you can get the audiobook version free with a free 30 days Audible trial.

Please follow the below *bit.ly* links based on where you reside.

US: *bit.ly/MLJ_Proverbs_US*

UK: *bit.ly/MLJ_Proverbs_UK*

France: *bit.ly/MLJ_Proverbs_FR*

Germany: *bit.ly/MLJ_Proverbs_DE*

All other countries: *bit.ly/MLJ_Proverbs_Others*

Ecclesiastes with God's Wisdom: Navigate life wisely with 30+ quotes & proverbs of wisdom from the Biblical book of Ecclesiastes

If you are new to Audible you can get the audiobook version of this book free with a free 30 days Audible trial.

Please follow the below *bit.ly* links based on where you reside.

US: *bit.ly/MLJ_Ecclesiastes_US*

UK: *bit.ly/MLJ_ Ecclesiastes_UK*

France: *bit.ly/MLJ_ Ecclesiastes_FR*

Germany: *bit.ly/MLJ_ Ecclesiastes_DE*

All other countries: *bit.ly/MLJ_Ecclesiastes_Others*

Made in the USA
Las Vegas, NV
24 August 2022